Better Homes and Gardens®

christmas

ornaments to make

Better Homes and Gardens® Books
Des Moines, Iowa

Better Homes and Gardens® Books
An imprint of Meredith® Books

Christmas Ornaments to Make

Editor: Carol Field Dahlstrom
Contributing Writer: Susan M. Banker
Graphic Designer: Angela Haupert Hoogensen
Copy Chief: Terri Fredrickson
Copy and Production Editor: Victoria Forlini
Editorial Operations Manager: Karen Schirm
Managers, Book Production: Pam Kvitne, Marjorie J. Schenkelberg
Contributing Copy Editor: Margaret Smith
Contributing Proofreaders: Maria Duryeé, Jessica Kearney Heidgerken, Beth Lastine
Photographers: Bill Hopkins, Peter Krumhardt, Scott Little, Andy Lyons Cameraworks
Technical Illustrator: Chris Neubauer Graphics, Inc.
Electronic Production Coordinator: Paula Forest
Editorial and Design Assistants: Kaye Chabot, Mary Lee Gavin, Karen McFadden

Meredith® Books
Editor in Chief: James D. Blume
Design Director: Matt Strelecki
Managing Editor: Gregory H. Kayko

Director, Sales, Special Markets: Rita McMullen
Director, Sales, Premiums: Michael A. Peterson
Director, Sales, Retail: Tom Wierzbicki
Director, Book Marketing: Brad Elmitt
Director, Operations: George A. Susral
Director, Production: Douglas M. Johnston

Vice President and General Manager: Douglas J. Guendel

***Better Homes and Gardens*® Magazine**
Editor in Chief: Karol DeWulf Nickell

Meredith Publishing Group
President, Publishing Group: Stephen M. Lacy
Vice President-Publishing Director: Bob Mate

Meredith Corporation
Chairman and Chief Executive Officer: William T. Kerr

Chairman of the Executive Committee: E. T. Meredith III

Library of Congress Control Number: 2002102024
ISBN: 0-696-21429-6

All of us at Better Homes and Gardens® Books are dedicated to providing you with information and ideas to create beautiful and useful projects. We welcome your comments and suggestions. Write to us at: Better Homes and Gardens Books, Crafts Editorial Department, 1716 Locust Street—LN112, Des Moines, IA 50309-3023.

If you would like to purchase any of our crafts, cooking, gardening, home improvement, or home decorating and design books, check wherever quality books are sold. Or visit us at: bhgbooks.com

Cover Photograph: Andy Lyons Cameraworks

Make your evergreen magical

We love it all! We love the holiday music, the handmade gifts, the friends who come to call—even the hustle and bustle. But it is the magnificent evergreen trimmed with ornaments that makes Christmas come alive. When the tree is up and decorated with dozens of colorful trims, we know Christmas is here. What better way to add to a glorious tradition than to make decorations to adorn that wonderful tree.

Handmade ornaments come in all shapes and sizes and can be tailored to suit each one of your family and friends. Some may prefer elegant or golden trims while others may enjoy childlike images or trims of all one color. Ornaments are round, shapely or flat, large or tiny. They can be painted, stitched, glittered, folded, molded, baked, drawn, jeweled, or carved. Whatever the style chosen, if an ornament is handmade, it is surely loved and treasured each year it returns to its special place on the tree.

In this book of Christmas ornaments, we've given you idea after idea for creating the perfect decoration to make for that special person or to hang on that unique tree. You'll find every color, a sleigh full of techniques, and even some unusual trims that will make you smile.

On those special nights before the big day arrives, sit down for a minute and watch the lights twinkling on that magical evergreen. As they cast their glow on your precious ornaments, may they remind you of the beauty of this glorious season. Merry Christmas!

Table of Contents

Exceptionally Elegant

Make your Christmas tree sparkle with elegant handcrafted ornaments. From golden crocheted edging and silver bargello stitches to glistening glitter dots and jewel-tone rhinestone accents, discover a sleighful of ornament ideas in this inspiring chapter.

What You'll Need

Metallic matte-finish ornament
Cup to hold ornament
Rhinestones in assorted jewel tones
Fine gold glitter
Thick white crafts glue

What To Do

1 Carefully place the clean ornament in the cup.

2 Glue rhinestones randomly on one side of ornament. Let dry. Rotate ornament; repeat. Let dry.

3 Apply fine lines of glue in a starburst pattern around each rhinestone on one side of ornament. Sprinkle each with glitter. Let dry. Repeat on other side of ornament. Let dry.

Sparkling Jeweled Trim

Round jewel-tone rhinestones set atop sparkling glitter stars add dimension to this pretty ornament. As it reflects the Christmas tree lights, this holiday trim will radiate with starbursts of vibrant color.

Metallic Pears

Too pretty to eat, these artificial pears are coated with metallic paint and highlighted with rhinestones. Display them in a pretty compote for a beautiful holiday centerpiece.

What You'll Need

Artificial pears
Masking tape
Newspapers
Metallic spray paints in desired colors (available at hobby stores)
Thick white crafts glue
Rhinestones to match colors of metallic paint
Gold acrylic paint
Paintbrush
Clear glass compote
¼-inch-wide ribbon
Scissors

What To Do

1 Mask off the pear leaves. In a well-ventilated work area, cover work surface with newspapers. Spray-paint the pears and let dry. Remove the masking tape.

2 Glue matching rhinestones in a triangle shape at the neck of the pear to resemble a highlight. Let dry. Add a highlight of gold paint to the leaf using a paintbrush. Allow to dry. Arrange pears in a small glass compote.

3 Cut a 12-inch-long piece of ribbon. Tie it to the stem for as trim or knot the ends for a hanger.

Delicately painted flowers lend charm to ordinary round ornaments.

Bands of Blooms

What You'll Need

Plain matte-finish ornaments
Pencil
Glass paint, such as Liquitex Glossies
Disposable plate; paintbrushes
Fine gold glitter (optional)
Rhinestones in desired colors
Thick white crafts glue
Cup to hold ornament

What To Do

1 Indicate placement for each flower with a pencil dot.

2 Put paint on a plate. Paint free-form large, small, pointed, or round petals around the dot. Paint one side of the ornament at a time, placing it in the cup to dry. Repeat to paint the other side. Let dry.

3 Paint a series of dashes between the flowers. Sprinkle with glitter if desired. Let dry. Glue three rhinestones in each flower center. Let dry. Turn the ornament in the cup with the top up. If desired, add a curvy line of glue around the top and sprinkle with glitter. Let dry.

Gilded Dewdrop

Glistening with glitter polka dots, make this quick ornament in any color combination to coordinate with your holiday decorating. Make a few extras to share your creativity with loved ones this Christmas.

WHAT YOU'LL NEED

Plain matte-finish ornaments
Scissors; 1/8-inch metallic ribbon
Thick white crafts glue; pencil
Fine gold glitter
Small cup to hold ornament

WHAT TO DO

1 Remove the ornament topper. Cut three lengths of ribbon, each long enough to wrap around the ornament. Glue the ribbons in place, using the photo, *below*, for placement. Replace the topper. Tie a ribbon bow around the hanger.

2 Working one section at a time, dot glue onto ornament with the eraser end of a pencil, then sprinkle with glitter. Set in a cup to dry. Repeat for each section.

As pretty as a stained glass window, this vivid design resembles a hot-air balloon. Gold beads add dimension to the colorful glittered points.

Hot-Air Balloon

What You'll Need

Large gold matte-finish ornament
Cup to hold ornament; pencil
Thick white crafts glue
Fine glitter in gold, green, pink, red, and blue; two small paintbrushes; small gold beads
Scissors; ½-inch-wide gold ribbon

What To Do

1 Place ornament, top up, in cup. Referring to photo, *above*, and using a pencil, make evenly spaced dots around the top of the ornament indicating the start of each line.

2 Draw lines with glue starting at each dot to about 2 inches down the ball. Make a "V" at the bottom of each set of lines. Sprinkle gold glitter over wet glue. Let dry. Turn the ball to the side and continue to draw glue diamonds extending from the top. Sprinkle with gold glitter. Let dry.

3 Use a paintbrush to brush away any loose glitter. Using the other paintbrush, brush glue between one set of lines at the ornament top. Sprinkle with colored glitter. Let dry before moving to the next area.

4 Glue a bead at the tip of each colored glitter section. Let dry. Thread ribbon through hanger. Knot ends to hang.

Holly Star

Made in pastel tones of traditional red and green, this machine-stitched star will be cherished for generations. Attach holly trims on each star point and jingling bells in the center. Metallic gold stitches add crisp detail.

What You'll Need

10-inch square of fusible transweb paper; pencil; pinking shears
10-inch squares of imitation suede in pink and green; scissors
Gold metallic machine thread
4 gold jingle bells; needle
5 sew-on holly trims; gold cord

What To Do

1 Trace and rotate the star point pattern five times on the fusible transweb paper. Fuse to back of pink suede. Cut out star using pinking shears. Cut out holly leaves in center.

2 Layer the pink star over the green suede. Machine-stitch around the outer edge of the pink star. Using the photograph, *opposite*, as a guide, zigzag-stitch veins on each holly leaf. Straight-stitch around and between holly cutouts.

3 Hand-sew jingle bells in the center of the ornament and a metal holly trim on each star point.

4 Use pinking shears to trim the green suede just beyond the edge of the pink suede. Sew a cord hanger to the back of one star point.

Holly Star Point Pattern

Holly Star Assembly Diagram

Rosebud Wreath

Simple, yet stunning, these ribbon wreaths work up quickly, so you can make one for everyone on your holiday gift list. Use the color scheme shown, or vary the color combination to create wreaths in a rainbow of hues.

WHAT YOU'LL NEED

1 yard of 2½-inch-wide bias-cut hand-dyed silk ribbon
1 yard of ½-inch piping cord
Thread to match color of ribbon
Needle
½ yard of silk ribbon cord
Nine ½-inch purchased silk ribbon flowers
Thick white crafts glue
Narrow gold ribbon

WHAT TO DO

1 Fold ribbon in half, wrong sides together, with piping cord inside along folded edge. Stitch with zipper foot attachment. Pull up thread to gather ribbon over 9 to 10 inches of cord.

2 Hand-stitch cord into a circle. Stitch ends of ribbon together over ends of piping. Attach a small ribbon cord bow to cover seam.

3 Arrange ribbon flowers in groups of three and glue to front. Let dry. Attach a gold ribbon hanging loop to the top back side of the ornament.

Holiday Cone

Embellished with a purchased appliqué, this cone ornament is large enough to fill with candies, a small gift, or holiday greenery. Find sequined appliqués in the bridal or holiday trim section of fabric stores.

Instructions are on page 20.

Holiday Cone *continued*

What You'll Need

Tracing paper
Pencil
Scissors
10-inch square of card stock
10-inch square of red velveteen fabric
Thick white crafts glue
Paper clip
Spray mount glue; gold cord
12 inches of 1-inch-wide double-face green satin ribbon, gathered along one edge
Purchased sequin appliqué trim
Jingle bell

What To Do

1 Enlarge and trace the pattern, *below*. Cut out shape. Trace around cone pattern on card stock and velveteen fabric. Cut out.

2 Roll the card stock shape into a cone, overlapping the ends as shown on the pattern. Secure with glue. Paper-clip the ends in place until the glue is dry. Remove the paper clip.

3 Spray the back side of the velveteen with spray mount glue. Allow to get tacky. Place the velveteen around the paper cone, overlapping the ends. Use crafts glue if necessary to secure the velveteen in place. Let dry.

4 Cut a 10-inch length of cord. Glue the ends to opposite sides inside the top of the cone. Let dry. Glue ruffle trim around the inside of the cone opening. Glue the appliqué on the cone, opposite the seam. Let dry. Use cord to tie a jingle bell to the bottom.

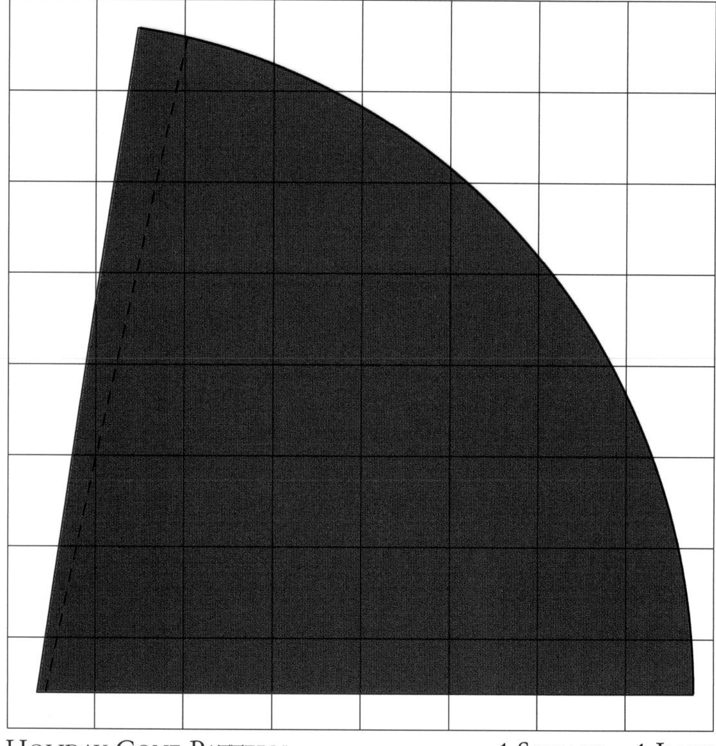

Holiday Cone Pattern — 1 Square = 1 Inch

Petals link to blanket this ornament with a lacy design. Coated with two colors of glitter and accented with tiny golden beads, this ornament is destined to become a treasured family favorite.

Glittered Lace Ornaments

WHAT YOU'LL NEED

Plain matte-finish round ornament
Small cup to hold ornament
Thick white crafts glue
Fine glitter in two colors
Small gold metallic beads

WHAT TO DO

1 Place the ornament in the cup. Work on one side of the ornament at a time. Referring to the photo, *above,* use glue to draw petals starting at the top of the ornament. At the end of each petal add more petals, having three or four petals meet in the center.

2 Sprinkle glitter over the wet glue. Add dimension by layering on a contrasting color of glitter. For example, lightly dust lavender glitter over green glitter. Let dry. Move to another area and add a group of four more petals. Sprinkle with glitter. Repeat until covered with lacy petals. Let dry.

3 Glue gold beads where the petals meet. Let dry.

Bargello Beauties

Stitched with a zigzag bargello needlepoint stitch, this pretty Christmas tree wears several shades of one color.

What You'll Need

One skein each of four coordinating shades of 3-ply wool needlepoint yarn
No. 5 metallic silver perle cotton
7×8-inch piece of interlock No. 10 needlepoint canvas; tracing paper
Pencil; fusible transweb paper
6×7-inch piece of matching imitation suede; scissors
Pinking shears; needle; mat board
Fabric glue; three 13mm jingle bells
Press cloth

What To Do

1 Use a 3-ply strand of wool for each of the four shades and three strands of metallic perle cotton to work the needlepoint bargello pattern. Start from the widest complete row at the bottom according to the diagram, *right*. Work a basket weave trunk as shown, *right*.

2 Enlarge and trace tree pattern, *right*, onto transweb paper. Fuse to wrong side of suede using a press cloth. Cut out suede ½ inch beyond design using pinking shears. Cut a tree shape from mat board.

3 Center and glue the mat board tree to the wrong side of the suede. Lightly steam wrong side of bargello with press cloth.

4 Cut out bargello tree allowing one canvas thread next to the stitching. Center and glue to suede.

5 For cord, cut 2½-yard pieces of one yarn color and of metallic perle cotton. Knot one end of the strands. Twist the strands together clockwise until they kink back on themselves. Fold the strand in half, knotting the fold. Twist the two strands counterclockwise to make cording. Tie ends. Glue cord around tree edges, as shown, *opposite*. Gather and secure cord to top of tree. Sew jingle bells at tree tip. Glue a suede tree shape to wrong side of ornament.

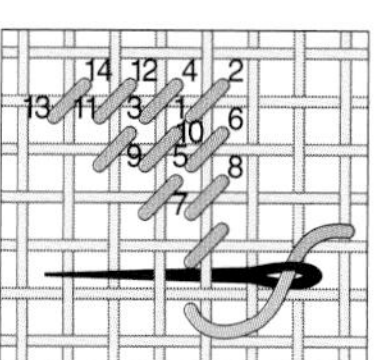

Basket Weave

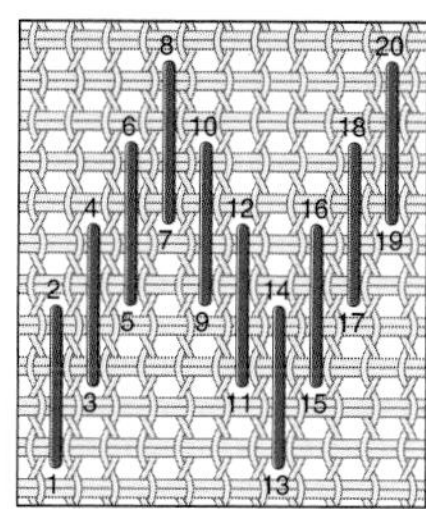

Bargello Stitch

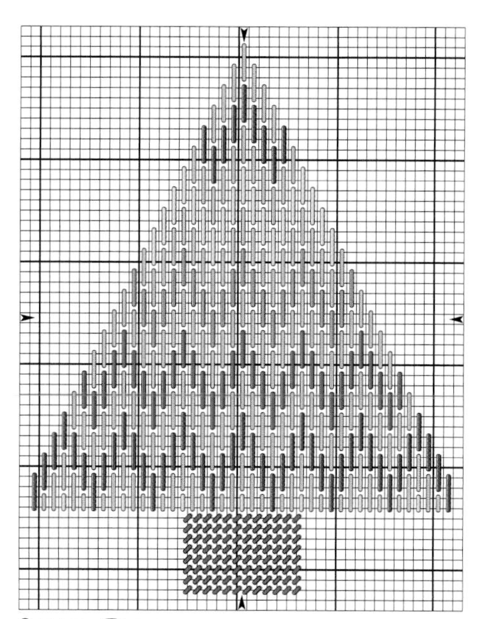

Stitch Diagram

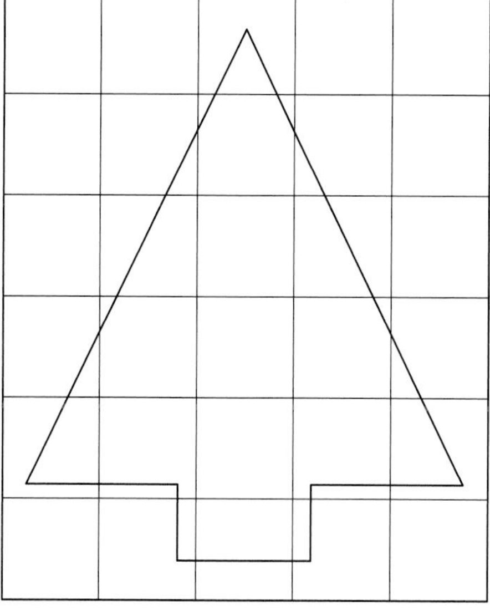

Bargello Tree Pattern 1 Square = 1 Inch

Victorian Cherub

Grandma will love these Victorian look-alikes. Back the trims with crepe paper and tinsel to replicate those from the early 1800s.

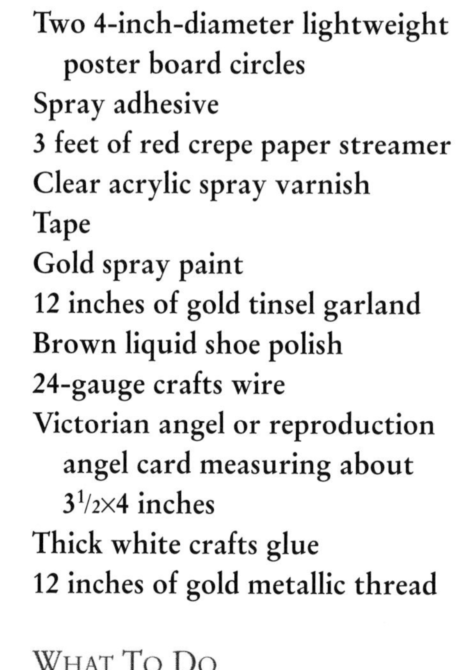

WHAT YOU'LL NEED

Two 4-inch-diameter lightweight poster board circles
Spray adhesive
3 feet of red crepe paper streamer
Clear acrylic spray varnish
Tape
Gold spray paint
12 inches of gold tinsel garland
Brown liquid shoe polish
24-gauge crafts wire
Victorian angel or reproduction angel card measuring about $3^{1}/_{2}$×4 inches
Thick white crafts glue
12 inches of gold metallic thread

WHAT TO DO

1 Glue poster board circles back to back using spray adhesive. Cut crepe paper streamer in half lengthwise. Tape one end of one crepe paper strip to one side of circle at center. Wrap streamer around circle, lapping edges in a spiral to cover the poster board circle. While wrapping, stretch crepe paper snug without bending the circle. Tape crepe paper end at center.

ANTIQUE ORNAMENT

2 Spray entire circle with varnish; allow to dry. Spray lightly with gold paint.

3 Trim fringe on tinsel garland to ½ inch wide. Rub brown shoe polish over garland for an antique look; let dry. Arrange garland on crepe paper circle as desired and glue in place. Glue angel card to circle over the garland.

4 Poke a small hole in the top of the ornament. Tie gold thread through the hole for a hanging loop.

REPRODUCTION ORNAMENT

Nature's Beauty

Milkweed pod poinsettias and pinecone blooms nestled in gold bows and white-as-snow leaves add interest and texture to evergreen branches. Metallic gold accents shimmer among these natural beauties.

Instructions are on page 28.

Nature's Beauty *continued*

WHAT YOU'LL NEED

Dried milkweed pods
Pinecones
Large tapioca
Newspapers
Gold spray paint
Transparent glass or floral spray paints in cranberry, orange-red, and green
Artificial leaves
White acrylic paint
Paintbrush
Gold paint marker
Hot-glue gun
Hot-glue sticks
1-inch metallic gold ribbon
Scissors

WHAT TO DO

1 Remove any remaining fluffy insides from dried milkweed pods. In a well-ventilated work area, place milkweed pods, large tapioca, and pinecones on newspapers. Spray all pieces gold. Let dry. Turn pieces over and spray other side. Let dry. Spray on a second coat if needed. Let dry.

2 Spray milkweed pods and pinecones with cranberry and orange-red paints. Spray some milkweed pods green for leaves. Paint artificial leaves white. Let dry. Outline leaves with a gold marker.

3 *For each poinsettia,* hot-glue five red milkweed pods together. Add one to three green milkweed pod leaves. Let dry. Hot-glue gold-painted tapioca clusters in the center of each flower. Let dry.

4 *For each pinecone,* cut a 12-inch length of ribbon. Tie the ribbon into a bow. Glue a pinecone and one or two white leaves in the center of the bow. Let dry.

Strings of Fancy

To trim a tree, grace a mantel, frame a doorway, or festoon a table, create one of these imaginative garlands for a personal touch.

WHAT YOU'LL NEED

Sheer ribbons in desired widths
Scissors
Wood beads and spools
Shell belt buckles
Starfish
Drill and ⅛-inch bit
Large-eyed needle
White acrylic paint
Paintbrush

WHAT TO DO

1 *For the bead and spool garland,* paint the wood pieces with two coats of white, letting each coat dry. String painted items on ribbon, knotting between items.

2 *For the buckle garland,* double one or two wide pieces of ribbon. The sample, *above,* has a double layer of white and cream 3-inch-wide ribbons. Weave the ribbons through the buckles.

3 *For the starfish garland,* drill a hole in one point of each starfish. Dry-brush stars with white paint. Let dry. Thread ribbon through needle. String starfish on ribbon.

Pleated Golden

Shimmering fabric and a lovely clip earring are used to make a keepsake ornament.

A

B

C

WHAT YOU'LL NEED

7×9-inches of pleated gold lamé
Thread
Needle
2-inch-long metallic gold tassel
3½-inch-diameter plastic foam ball, such as Styrofoam
18 inches of gold cording
Scissors
18 inches of 1-inch-wide pink ribbon
Clip earring or lapel pin

WHAT TO DO

1 Right sides together, sew short ends of lamé to make a tube. Hand-sew running stitches along top and bottom raw edges as shown in Photo A, *left,* and *below.* Gather bottom thread. From inside tube, push tassel hanger through gathers. Stitch to secure. Turn tube right side out.

2 Put the plastic foam ball inside the tube. Gather the running stitches. Cut a 6-inch length of gold cording for the hanger. Tuck the ends of the cording into the gathers. Stitch to secure as shown in Photo B.

3 Tie the ribbon into a bow over running stitches. Tie remaining cording into a bow beneath the ribbon bow. Clip or pin the jewelry piece to the center of the bows as shown in Photo C.

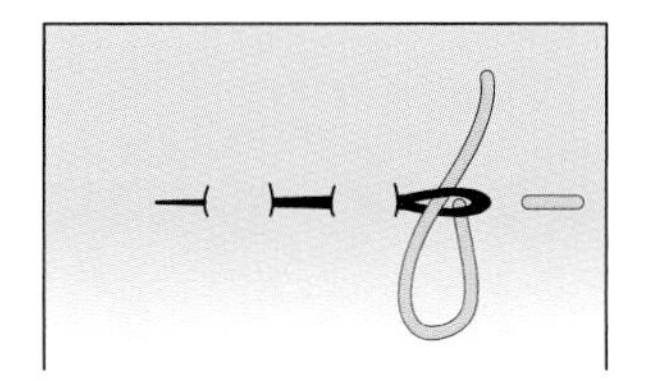

RUNNING STITCH

Ornament

Beaded-Fringe

As pretty as a gown for a winter gala, this pastel ornament glistens with a beaded skirt and jewel-like polka dots.

WHAT YOU'LL NEED

Cup to hold ornament; scissors
Purchased beaded fringe trim
Glass ball ornament in any pastel color; tape
Thick white crafts glue
Rhinestones to coordinate with ornament
Narrow ribbon
Clear pedestal-style candleholder

WHAT TO DO

1 Place the ornament in a cup to prevent rolling. Cut the beaded fringe trim to fit around the ornament. Glue the trim in place. If necessary, tape the trim while glue sets. (Test the tape on an area to ensure that it doesn't lift the finish from the ornament.) When dry, remove tape.

2 Glue the rhinestones randomly on the top half of the ornament. Let dry.

3 Thread ribbon through the hanger. Knot the ends together to hang. If desired, display the ornament in a clear candleholder.

Ornament

An endearing initial pin personalizes this lovely trim,

which is edged with sparkling gold crochet.

WHAT YOU'LL NEED

Metallic gold perle cotton
No. 0 steel crochet hook; scissors
4-inch square of red velveteen
2½-inch covered button kit
2¼-inch gold curtain ring with clip
Initial pin; ¼-inch-wide ribbon

WHAT TO DO

1 For crocheted edging, start at one side of curtain ring clip with No. 0 steel hook and metallic gold perle cotton. Work 66 sc around ring. Join with slip stitch. * Sc in next sc, hdc in next sc, 2 dc in next sc, 3 trc in next sc, 2 dc in next sc, hdc in next sc (see abbreviations, *page 56*). Rep from * around, completing 11 scallop patterns. Join to beg and secure ends.

2 Cover button with velveteen according to manufacturer's directions. Glue button to curtain ring. Pin an initial pin in center of ornament. Add ribbon hanger.

Personally Yours

M
R

Winter White

At Christmastime, capture the beauty of shimmering frosty mornings. The assortment of ornaments in this chapter will help you bedeck your holiday home in a dazzling blanket of white.

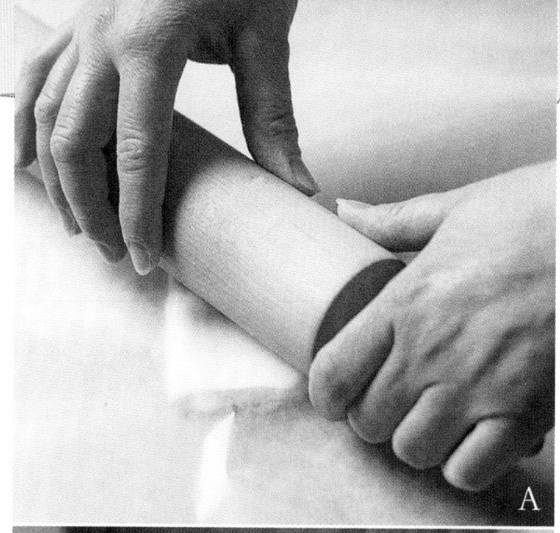

A

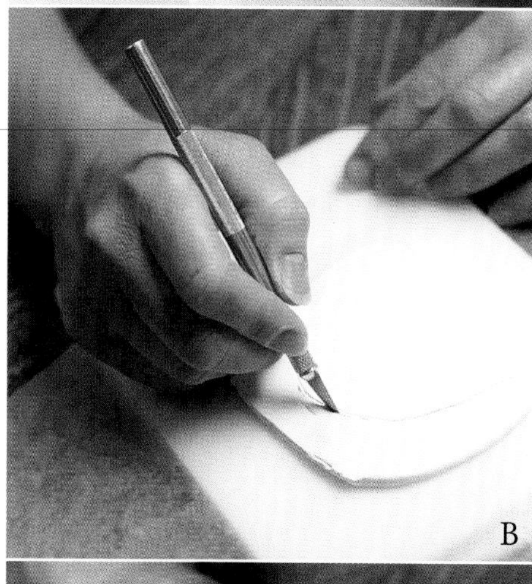

B

C

D

What You'll Need

Waxed paper; rolling pin
White oven-bake clay, such as Sculpey; tracing paper; pencil
Scissors; paper clip; wire cutter
Glass or metal baking pan
Crafts knife; cutting board; cord

What To Do

1 Place a golf-ball-size piece of clay between sheets of waxed paper. Use a rolling pin to flatten clay to ¼-inch thickness, as shown in Photo A. Trace the arched background pattern, *below right*, onto tracing paper. Cut out. Draw around the shape on the clay. Slide a cutting board under clay. Cut out the arched shape using a crafts knife as shown in Photo B.

2 Roll a long coil of clay to outline the arch of the background piece. Roll three coils to form the roof. Press onto edge of background piece as shown in Photo C.

3 Place a grape-size piece of clay on waxed paper. Roll to approximately ⅛-inch thick. Use a crafts knife to cut out a star. Press shape to top of roof.

4 Use a wire cutter to snip off the end of a paper clip to use as a hanging loop. Press the open end of the clip into the top of the roof (under the star).

5 Using the pattern, *below*, as a guide for placement and sizing, shape and add clay pieces. Make small ropes for the hay, robe accents, and halo. Press the pieces into place.

6 Bake clay in oven as directed by clay manufacturer. Let cool.

7 Using a crafts knife, carve away tiny pieces from the clay ornament to resemble wood carving, as shown in Photo D. Thread cord through the paper clip hanger. Knot the ends to hang.

Carved Nativity Pattern

Carved from clay, this snow-white nativity scene is a wondrous reminder of the first Christmas so long ago.

Carved Nativity

Winter Frost Trims

A touch of winter white is easy to mimic on etched glass ornaments.

WHAT YOU'LL NEED

Clear glass ornament
White vinegar
¼-inch-wide masking tape
White tube-style paint
Star stickers
Latex gloves
Etching cream
Paintbrush
Beaded extension chain
Sprig of greenery

What To Do

1 Wash ornament with hot water and white vinegar. Avoid touching the areas to be etched. Referring to the etched ornaments, *opposite* and *above* and in Photo A at *right*, use paint and/or masking tape to make designs. To make star shapes, press on star stickers. Rub tape and stickers to adhere to surface. Allow the paint to dry.

2 Put on latex gloves. Paint the ornament with etching cream (Photo B) following the manufacturer's directions. Leave the etching cream on for the recommended time.

3 Wash off the etching cream and gently peel off the paint and/or stickers and tape as shown in Photo C. Thread the extension chain through the ornament hanger and snap closed. Tuck a small sprig of greenery into the ornament top.

Frosted Leaves

In a few simple steps, you can re-create this snow-kissed bauble.

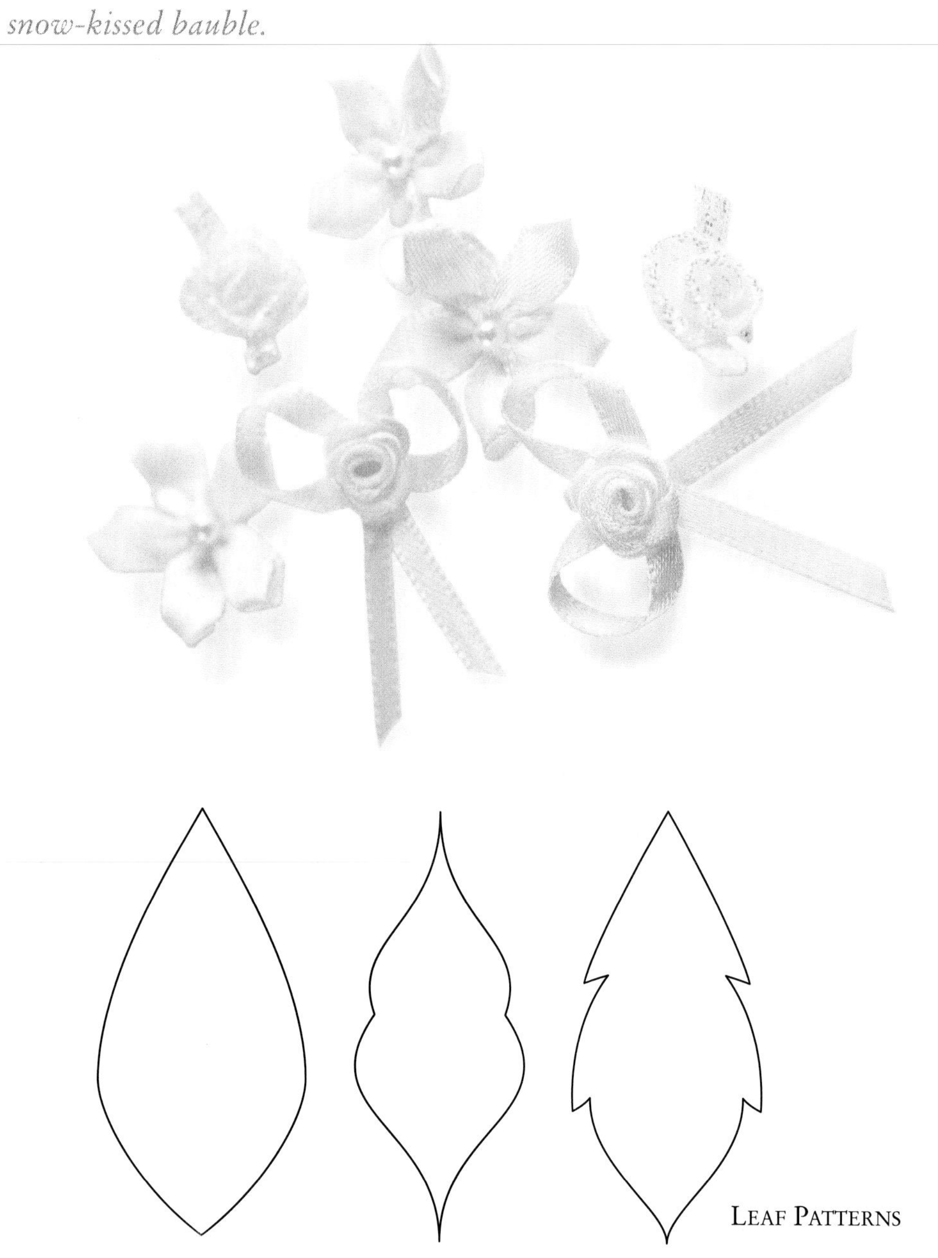

Leaf Patterns

What You'll Need

Pencil; tracing paper
Scissors
White iridescent paper
White glass ball ornament
Thick white crafts glue
White fabric paint
White glitter
White silk flowers
Cup to hold ornament
Ribbon for hanging

What To Do

1 Trace the desired leaf pattern, *below left*, onto tracing paper. Cut out and trace onto white paper five or six times. Cut out.

2 Glue the leaves vertically on the ornament. Outline the shapes with white fabric paint. While wet, sprinkle with white glitter. Let the glue and paint dry.

3 Glue small white flowers at tips of leaves. Place ornaments in a cup and let dry.

4 Thread ribbon through the hanger. Knot the ends together to hang.

Ornament

Beaded Initials

Exquisite on a package or reflecting the lights of the tree, these beaded letters give anything a personal touch.

WHAT YOU'LL NEED

16 to 18 inches of 18-gauge wire
Assorted beads; needle-nose pliers
Artificial greenery or holly
Gold cording or ribbon; scissors

WHAT TO DO

1 Enlarge and trace desired initial from alphabet pattern, *below*. Roll a tight loop at the end of the wire to prevent beads from sliding off as shown in the diagram, *below*. Bead wire in a pattern. Roll another loop at opposite end of wire.

2 Bend the wire to form a script letter, using the pattern as a guide. If the letter requires a cross wire, repeat the process with a shorter length and wire the beaded pieces together. Add large beads on wires to the wire ends, if desired.

3 Adorn the letter with a sprig of evergreen and tie on a hanging cord or ribbon.

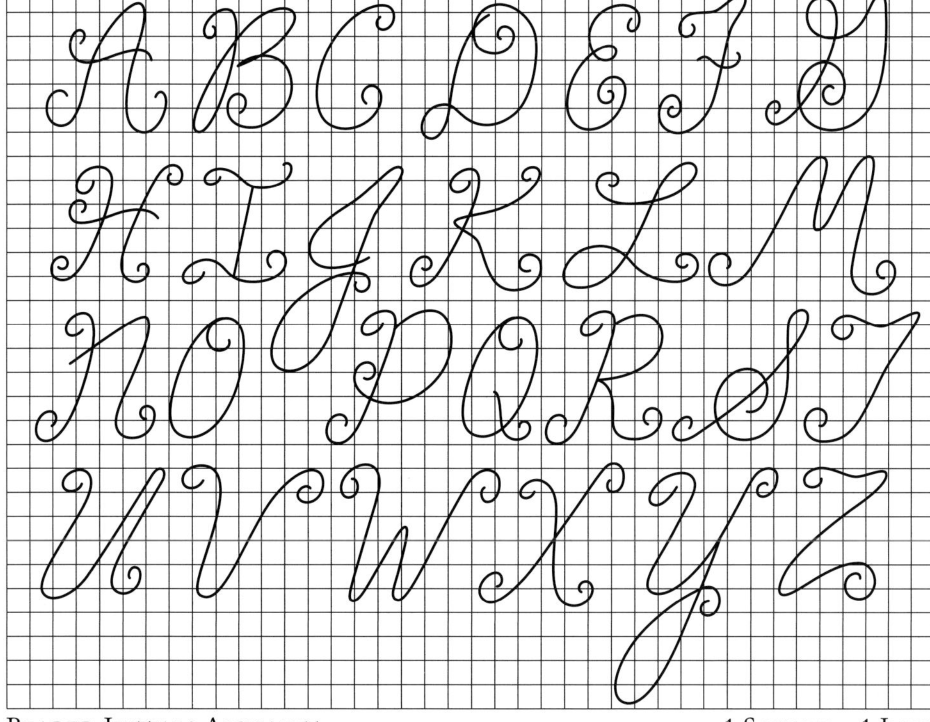

BEADED INITIALS ALPHABET 1 SQUARE = 1 INCH

BEADED INITIALS ASSEMBLY DIAGRAM

Pure white woolen fabric, beads, and glitter make these delicate snowflakes sparkle. Use the patterns on pages 48–49 or create your own shapes.

What You'll Need

Tracing paper; pencil; scissors
Heavy-weight fusible transweb paper
12 inches 1/8-inch-wide ribbon; iron
Medium-weight white wool
White glitter tube-style paint
1-inch crystal bugle star beads
3/8-inch clear plastic star beads
Large crystal seed beads; 1/2-inch sew-on white sequin snowflakes
White thread; beading needle
Paintbrush; white glitter paint

What To Do

1 Trace desired snowflake pattern, *pages 48–49,* onto tracing paper. Transfer to fusible transweb paper. Fuse to the wrong side of the wool fabric following the manufacturer's directions, as shown in Photo A.

2 Cut out the snowflake shape from the fused wool fabric as shown in Photo B.

3 Remove the backing from the transweb paper as shown in Photo C. Place ends of ribbon on webbing at top of snowflake, overlapping the edge about 1/2 inch to make a hanging loop. Fuse the snowflake shape to another piece of wool fabric so both the front and the back of the snowflake are wool.

4 Cut out the snowflake shape a second time, being careful to avoid cutting off the hanging loop as shown in Photo D.

5 Seal the edges of the snowflake with a paint pen, as shown in Photo E. Let the paint dry. Stitch beads and sequins to the snowflake as shown on the patterns. Paint the surface of the snowflake using a paintbrush and white glitter paint.

Winter Wool Snowflakes

Winter Wool Snowflake Pattern — Rounded Edge

Winter Wool Snowflake
Pattern — Pointed Edge

Snow-Kissed Trims

Whether flocked or polka-dotted, glittered or beaded, white ornaments are breathtaking nestled among Christmas greenery.

WHAT YOU'LL NEED FOR THE SWIRLED ORNAMENT

Liner paintbrush; white flocking kit, such as Soft Flock by Plaid
Clear glass ornament; toothpick
Strong adhesive, such as E6000
Small rhinestones; cup

WHAT TO DO

1 Using a brush and flock adhesive in kit, make small spirals on one side of the ornament.

2 While the adhesive is wet, dust white flocking powder over the spirals. Let dry in cup. Repeat for remaining side.

3 Use a toothpick to apply epoxy to rhinestone backs; center on spirals. Let dry. Add desired hanger.

WHAT YOU'LL NEED FOR THE STARS AND HEARTS ORNAMENT

White matte-finish ornament
Thick white crafts glue
White glitter
White confetti in star and heart shapes; cup

WHAT TO DO

1 Using glue, draw curlicues extending from ornament top. Sprinkle with glitter. Let dry. Glue on confetti. Let dry. Add hanger.

WHAT YOU'LL NEED FOR THE FEATHERED ORNAMENT

Matte-finish silver ornament
White hole-punch reinforcements and white round labels
Thick white crafts glue
Liner paintbrush
Fine white glitter; white feathers
Needle; white thread; cup

WHAT TO DO

1 Apply round stickers randomly to ornament. Dilute glue with water; apply a coat to stickers. While wet, sprinkle glitter on glue, working from top to bottom. Let dry in cup.

2 Use a needle and thread to tack the ends of a feather scrap together. Slip feather collar over ornament cap. Add desired hanger.

WHAT YOU'LL NEED FOR THE BEADED ORNAMENT

Strong adhesive, such as E6000
Scissors
Silver ribbon and trim
Matte-finish silver ornament
Seed beads in silver and clear
Toothpick; cup

WHAT TO DO

1 Glue trim around the ornament approximately ½ inch below cap, overlapping ends. Repeat with additional ribbon and trim, leaving about ⅜ inch between trims. Glue trim around the metal cap. Let dry.

2 Use a toothpick to apply dots of adhesive centered between ribbons and trim; press alternating beads into glue. Let dry.

Swirled Ornament

Stars and Hearts Ornament

Feathered Ornament

Beaded Ornament

These symbols of winter add festive flair to a Christmas tree, package, or chandelier. Complement the snowflakes with white ribbon bows, baby's breath, and paper birds.

Crocheted Snowflakes

Instructions are on pages 54-56.

Crocheted Snowflakes

Just like the real thing, these delicate crocheted snowflakes confirm that no two are exactly alike.

WHAT YOU'LL NEED

DMC Cébélia white crochet thread, size 30
No. 10 steel crochet hook
White glue
Rustproof pins
Aluminum foil
Cardboard

NOTE: *Crochet abbreviations are on page 56.*

HOW TO MAKE SNOWFLAKE 1

Diameter is 4¼ inches.

1 Ch 8; join with sl st to form ring.

2 **Rnd 1:** Ch 1, 18 sc in ring; join with sl st to first sc.

3 **Rnd 2:** *Ch 12, sl st in fifth ch from hook; working a sl st in first ch of each of the next 10-ch lps, (ch 10, sl st, ch 5, sl st) twice; ch 16, sl st; (ch 5, sl st, ch 10, sl st) twice; ch 5 sl st; then sl st in base of first ch-5 lp; sl st in next 7 chs and in same st as beg ch-12 lp; ch 12, sl st in same st as last sl st; sl st in next 3 sc, ch 12, sl st in same st as last sl st. Rep from * 5 times more. Fasten off.

HOW TO MAKE SNOWFLAKE 2

Diameter is 4½ inches.

1 Ch 7; join with sl st to form ring.

2 **Rnd 1:** Ch 1, 12 sc in ring; join with sl st to first sc.

3 **Rnd 2:** *Ch 16, sl st in seventh ch from beg and in next 6 ch, sc in same st at base of ch; sc in next st, ch 30, sl st in seventh ch from beg; (ch 24, sl st in third ch from beg) twice; sl st in next 2 chs; ch 22, sl st in first ch from beg of ch; sl st in next 2 ch (of main stem); ch 24, sl st in first ch of beg ch; sl st in rem 6 ch to base of stem, sc in same sc on ring, sc in next sc on ring. Rep from * 5 times more; join to first ch at beg of first stem; fasten off.

ch 12, sl st; ch 10, sl st; ch 14, sl st; sl st in base of first ch-14 lp, sl st in next ch, in dtr, in next 12 ch, and in next sc; rep from * around; end sl st in last 12 ch and in same st as beg ch-8. Fasten off.

How To Make Snowflake 3

Diameter is 5¼ inches.

1 Ch 8, join with sl st to form ring.

2 **Rnd 1:** Ch 1, 24 sc in ring; join to first sc.

3 **Rnd 2:** Ch 5, (sk sc, dc in next sc, ch 2) 11 times; join to third ch of beg ch 5.

4 **Rnd 3:** Ch 1, in each ch-2 lp around work 3 sc; join to first sc.

5 **Rnd 4:** ** Ch 6, sk 2 sc, sc in next sc; ch 9, yo hook twice, draw up lp in sixth ch from hook, (yo draw through 2 lps on hook) twice; *yo hook twice, draw up lp in same ch, rep bet ()s twice; rep from * once more; yo, draw through rem 4 lps on hook—trc cluster (cl) made; ch 6, sl st in base of cl, ch 3, sk 2 sc, sc in next sc. Rep from ** 5 times more; join last ch-3 to first ch of beg ch-6.

6 **Rnd 5:** Sl st in next 2 ch, * ch 12, yo hook 3 times, draw up lp in top of trc-cl, (yo draw through 2 lps on hook) 4 times—dtr made; dtr in top of trc-cl, ch 12, sc in next ch-6 lp. Rep from * 5 times more; join last ch in first ch of beg ch-12.

7 **Rnd 6:** *(Ch 8, sl st in third ch from beg of ch) twice; ch 12, sl st in first ch, (ch 6, sl st in first ch; sl st in base of opposite ch-lp and in each of next 2 ch) twice; sl st in same st as join, in each of next 11 ch, and in dtr. Working a sl st in second ch from beg of ch in each of next ch-lps, ch 14, sl st; ch 10, sl st,

How To Make Snowflake 4

Diameter is 4¾ inches.

1 Ch 10, join with sl st to form ring.

2 **Rnd 1:** Ch 4, ** trc in ring, ch 1, dtr in ring; ch 9, sl st in third ch from hook and in each of next 6 ch, sl st in dtr, ch 1, trc in ring, ch 1 *; dc in ring, ch 1, rep from ** 5 times more, ending last rep at *; join last ch-1 to third ch of beg ch-4; fasten off.

3 **Rnd 2:** Join thread in any ch-3 lp at tip of any stem; * ch 12, sl st in ninth ch from hook—first ch-8 lp made; ch 1, trc in same ch-3 lp, ch 10, sl st in last trc; ch 1, trc in ch-3

continued on page 56

lp, ch 12, sl st in last trc; ch 1, trc in ch-3 lp, ch 14, sl st in last trc; ch 1, trc in ch-3 lp, ch 12, sl st in last trc; ch 1, trc in ch-3 lp, ch 10, sl st in last trc; ch 1, trc in ch-3 lp, ch 8, sl st in last trc; ch 6, trc in ch-3 lp at tip of next stem; rep from * 5 times more; join last ch-6 with sl st to base of first ch-8 lp at beg of rnd; fasten off.

How To Make Snowflake 5

Diameter is 5¼ inches.

1 Ch 8; join with sl st to form ring.

2 **Rnd 1:** Ch 3, 17 dc in ring; join with sl st to top of beg ch-3.

3 **Rnd 2:** Ch 1, sc in same st as join, * ch 8, sk 2 dc, sc in next dc. Rep from * 5 times; sl st last ch-8 to first sc.

4 **Rnd 3:** In each ch-8 lp work 10 sc; join with sl st to first sc.

5 **Rnd 4:** *Working sl st in fourth ch from beg in each of following 9-ch lengths, ch 18, sl st; ch 16, sl st; ch 14, sl st; (ch 12, sl st) 3 times; ch 14, sl st; ch 16, sl st; ch 18, sl st; ch 3, sc in same st as join or last sc, (ch 7, sl st in fourth ch from hook) 5 times; ch 3, sk 9 sc, sc in next sc. Rep from * 5 times. Join last ch-3 in same sc as beg ch-8. Fasten off.

How to Finish Snowflakes:

Use a piece of foam-core board to lay out the ornaments. Unless the board has a glazed or plastic finish, cover it with waxed paper or aluminum foil. Use one of the following methods to stiffen the ornaments:

Starch

Using liquid or spray starch to stiffen ornaments will enable you to wash them.

Follow the package directions to prepare cooked starch for a very stiff finish. Dip ornament into solution; press out excess starch between paper towels.

Lay ornament on work surface; pin symmetrically from center out. Position each spoke straight from center. Shape loops and picots to a pleasing design.

To use spray starch, first dampen the ornament with water. Pin out the ornament and saturate with spray starch. Let dry; repeat until the ornament is stiff.

White Glue

Ornaments stiffened with glue can be cleaned with a damp rag or soft brush.

Mix a solution of ⅔ glue and ⅓ water. Dip ornament into solution and shape.

Crochet Abbreviations

beg...begin(ning)
ch...chain
cl...cluster
dc...double crochet
dec...decrease
dtr...double treble
hdc...half double crochet
inc...increase
lp(s)...loop(s)
pc...popcorn
rem...remaining
rep...repeat
rnd(s)...round(s)
sc...single crochet
sl...slip
sp...space
st...stitch
sk...skip
trc...treble crochet
yo...yarn over

Chunky glitter adds lacy white-on-white dimension to these teardrop ornaments. Hang them on the tree with sheer ribbon or place them in a cut-glass bowl to grace a side table.

Snowy Teardrops

WHAT YOU'LL NEED

White matte-finish teardrop-shape ornaments
White tube-style paint
Large diameter white glitter
Small towel (optional)

WHAT TO DO

1 Refer to the patterns, *below*, for design ideas. Work on one side of the ornament at a time. With the paint, draw large and small snowflakes on the ornaments as desired.

2 While the paint is wet, sprinkle on glitter. Let paint dry. To prevent the ornament from rolling, lay it in the center of a small towel while working on it and while it dries.

SNOWFLAKE PATTERNS

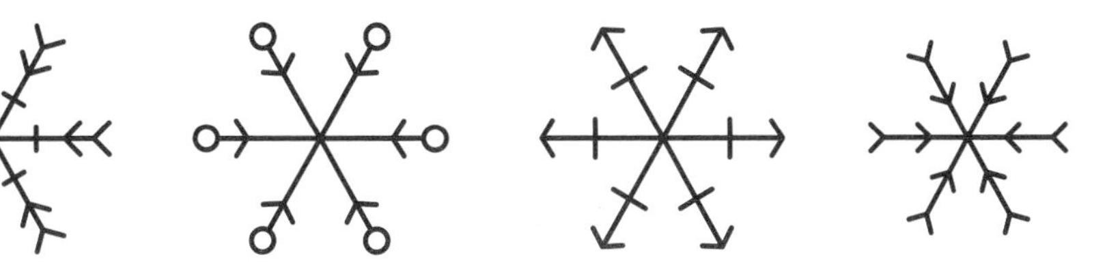
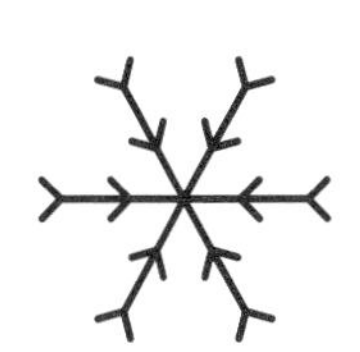

Dressed-in-White Angel

Make dozens of these heavenly trims with coffee filter gowns and wings. Finish the cherubs with golden ribbon and tiny ring halos.

WHAT YOU'LL NEED

3 coffee filters
3½-inch foam cone, such as Styrofoam
1 round toothpick
1-inch foam ball, such as Styrofoam
12 inches of ¼-inch-wide gold ribbon
White thread; hot-glue gun and glue sticks
1 gold plastic ring

WHAT TO DO

1 Center a coffee filter on the top of the cone. Push the toothpick three-quarters of the way into the cone and filter. Push the 1-inch ball onto the toothpick for the head.

2 Center the second filter on the head. Tie a ribbon bow around the neck.

3 Fold the third filter in half and pleat it at the center to form wings. Tie in the center with thread. Hot-glue the center of the wings to the back of the angel at the neck. Glue the ring to the top of the head for a halo.

Perfect for a winter wedding gift or to hang on an all-white tree, this dainty ornament works up quickly, making it a candidate for last-minute creations.

Lovely Lace Trim

WHAT YOU'LL NEED

2 white lace trim motifs (available in fabric departments)
Thick white crafts glue; paintbrush
White matte-finish ornament
White glitter; white pearl beads
⅛-inch-wide white satin ribbon

WHAT TO DO

1 Apply glue to back of trim and rub in. Place on ornament.

2 Brush glue over lace. Sprinkle with glitter. Glue a cluster of pearl beads in center of flower portion of the lace. Let dry.

3 Make a wavy glue line around the ornament top. Sprinkle with glitter. Let dry.

4 Thread ribbon through the topper. Knot the ends.

Family Favorites

Gather the family together and craft some ornaments that you'll all love to make. From friendly elves and merry mittens to pasta bows and marble snowmen, the whole clan will smile at these fun-to-make trims.

Leaf Buddies

Put a twist on Mother Nature's ornaments by painting fallen leaves and adorning them with handmade bugs.

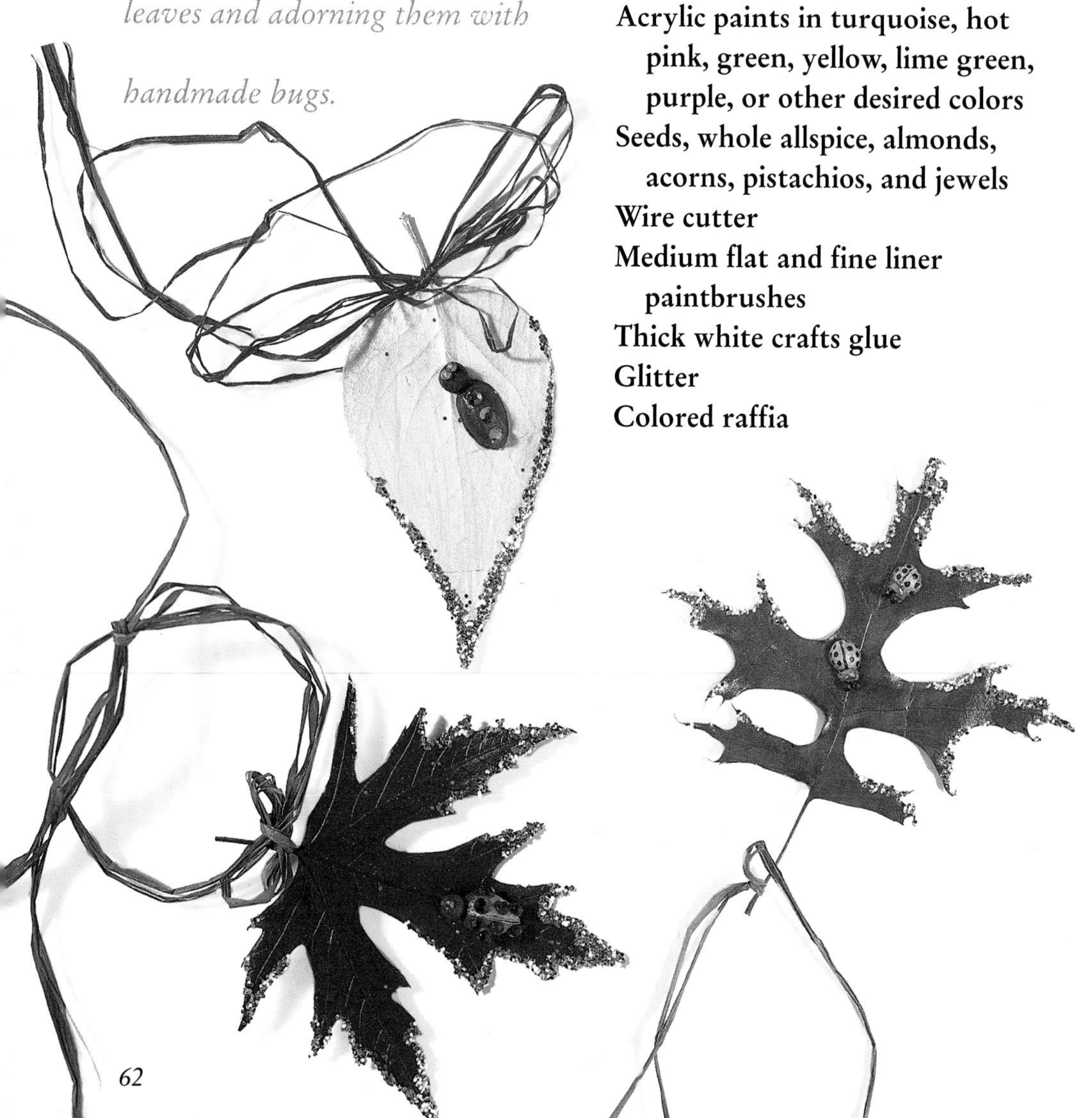

What You'll Need

Newspapers
Dried leaves
Spray primer
Acrylic paints in turquoise, hot pink, green, yellow, lime green, purple, or other desired colors
Seeds, whole allspice, almonds, acorns, pistachios, and jewels
Wire cutter
Medium flat and fine liner paintbrushes
Thick white crafts glue
Glitter
Colored raffia

What To Do

1. In a well-ventilated work area, cover work surface with newspapers. Lay leaves on newspapers and spray primer on one side. Let dry. Repeat for other side. Paint leaf desired color. Let dry. Repeat for other side.

2. Outline the leaf with glue. While the glue is wet, sprinkle glitter over the glue. Shake off the excess glitter and let the glue dry.

3. Create insects using almonds, acorns, whole allspice, coriander, pistachios, or other seeds and nuts. Cut the allspice in half with wire cutters, such as for the ladybugs. Paint the bug pieces before assembling. Let dry. To paint dots on the bugs, dip the paintbrush handle in paint and dot the surface. Let the paint dry.

4. Assemble bugs using glue. Glue rhinestones on insects if desired. Let dry. Glue the insects onto the leaves. Let dry.

5. Tie colored raffia to the stems of the leaves for hanging or tie the ornament to a jar to give as a gift.

BUGS

Button-Up Beauties

Decorate child-size mittens into country-style ornaments. Stiffen the mittens and embellish them with bead-and-button snowflakes.

Merry Mittens

WHAT YOU'LL NEED

Waxed paper; liquid fabric stiffener
Bowl; small mittens; buttons
Thread; needle; artificial holly
Hot-glue gun; hot-glue sticks
White tube-style paint
Ribbon; scissors

WHAT TO DO

1 Place waxed paper on a flat work surface. Pour fabric stiffener in a bowl. Dip the mittens in fabric stiffener. Lay the mittens on the waxed paper to dry.

2 Sew through buttons with thread. Arrange buttons in snowflake designs on the mitten fronts. Hot-glue the buttons in place. Paint snowflake lines. Let dry.

3 Cut an 8-inch length of ribbon. Stitch ends inside each mitten to form a loop. Tie two small ribbon bows. Hot-glue a sprig of holly and bows in place.

Buttons-in-a-Row Garland

WHAT YOU'LL NEED

Scissors; white embroidery floss
Needle; assorted buttons in white, green, and red
1½-inch-wide wire-edge red felt or velvet ribbon with decorative edge

WHAT TO DO

1 Thread embroidery floss through needle. Stack three different color buttons, from largest to smallest. Poke the needle through the top button and through each of the remaining two buttons. Wind the floss around the ribbon once and bring the needle back up through the stack of buttons. Knot the ends. Trim the floss ends to about ¼ inch.

2 Repeat to sew a stack of buttons approximately every 1½ inches to make the garland length.

Festive Finials

Trying to find a new look for your Christmas tree? Head to the home center. With a few easy steps, wood finials become colorful ornaments.

WHAT YOU'LL NEED

Newspapers
Wood finials
Spray primer
Acrylic paints in desired colors
Small paintbrush
Spray clear coat
Pliers
Small eye screws
Ribbon
Scissors

WHAT TO DO

1 In a well-ventilated work area, cover the work surface with newspapers. Spray the finials with a coat of primer. Let dry.

2 Paint designs on each finial, using the finial shape as a guide. Let the paint dry. In a well-ventilated work area, spray ornaments with protective clear coat. Let dry.

3 Remove the screw from the finial end with pliers and replace with an eye screw. Tie a ribbon on the screw to hang.

Beaded Banding

Bring personality to any color Christmas ball with ornate buttons, pearls, and beads. March them around the ornament as banding or place them randomly for pretty polka dots.

WHAT YOU'LL NEED

Rubber band
Round ornament
Strong adhesive, such as E6000
Toothpick
Buttons
Half-pearl beads
Round beads
Cup to hold ornament

WHAT TO DO

1 Place a rubber band on the ornament to keep the bottom edge of the button-bead design straight. Determine a button-bead pattern.

2 Using a toothpick, apply adhesive to buttons and beads to adhere to ornament. If gluing beads to the buttons, do so before applying the trim to the ornament. Place in a cup and let dry.

Pretty Pasta Trims

If you didn't save the macaroni trims you made when you were a kid, here's an updated version that seems like child's play.

WHAT YOU'LL NEED

Waxed paper
Thick white crafts glue
Gloss acrylic enamel paints in green, red, purple, turquoise, and yellow
Gold thread for hanging

FOR THE POINSETTIA

Pasta shells in medium and small
Couscous or small tubular bead-shape pasta

FOR THE BOW WITH STREAMERS

Bow tie pasta
Elbow macaroni
Elongated coiled pasta; small shells pasta

FOR THE WREATH

Medium-size tubular pasta
Bow tie pasta
Elbow macaroni
Black pipe cleaner

WHAT TO DO

1 Place waxed paper on a work surface. *For the poinsettia,* glue together small and medium shells. For the center, use a generous amount of glue to secure the couscous.

2 *For the bow with streamer ornament,* glue an elbow macaroni onto a bow shape. Glue elongated coiled pasta for streamers onto bow tie pasta and end with shells. Let glued pasta dry.

3 Paint all of the pieces for the poinsettia and bow with streamers purple. Let dry. Layer colors to create a more dimensional appearance, if desired. Paint reds over purple, and yellow over red, such as on the streamer tips. Paint green over purple for bow and leaves, and yellow over green, such as on the center of the poinsettia.

4 *For the wreath,* paint the tubes green and turquoise. Glue an elbow macaroni onto a bow pasta. Let dry. String the tubes onto a piece of black pipe cleaner. Tie the pipe cleaner into a wreath. Paint the bow tie pasta purple. Let dry. Paint red over the purple. Let dry. Glue the bow in place.

5 Tie gold thread to each ornament to hang.

Marble Snowmen

That lonely single knit glove may have found a happy home when its fingers adorn the top of these jolly fellows. Add a jingle bell and silly faces to make this winter trio.

WHAT YOU'LL NEED

Scissors
Knit gloves
White boulder marbles
Strong adhesive, such as E6000
Thread to match gloves
Darning needle
Small jingle bells
Orange oven-bake clay, such as Sculpey; glass baking dish
Black acrylic glass paint
Round toothpick
Silver cord

WHAT TO DO

1 For each snowman hat, cut a finger off a knit glove. Glue to a marble. Let dry.

2 Make a stitch or two in the tip of the hat to form a point. Sew a jingle bell to the point and stitch to the hat brim to secure.

3 Roll a tiny carrot-shape nose from clay. Bake on a glass baking dish in oven according to the clay manufacturer's directions. Let cool. Glue the nose in place. Let dry.

4 Dip a toothpick in black paint and dot on the marble for eyes and mouth. Let dry.

Scherenschnitte Garland

WHAT YOU'LL NEED

Tracing paper; pencil; scissors
Tea-dyed white felt

WHAT TO DO

1 Trace and cut out the pattern, *below.* Cut a 2×5½-inch strip from felt. Accordion-fold the strip to the width of the pattern. Trace around pattern on felt strip, aligning the folds.

2 Cut out the shapes, being careful not to cut through the folded areas. Unfold. Repeat to make desired number of strips.

Holly Garland

WHAT YOU'LL NEED

Tracing paper; pencil; scissors
Green wrapping paper
Paper punch
Red eyelets and eyelet tool

WHAT TO DO

1 Trace the holly pattern, *below.* Cut out. Cut a 4×12-inch strip from wrapping paper. Accordion-fold the strip to the width of the pattern. Trace around the pattern on the folded paper strip, aligning the folds.

2 Cut out holly shape, being careful not to cut through the folded areas. Unfold.

3 Use a paper punch to punch holes for holly berries from garland. Secure a red eyelet in each hole.

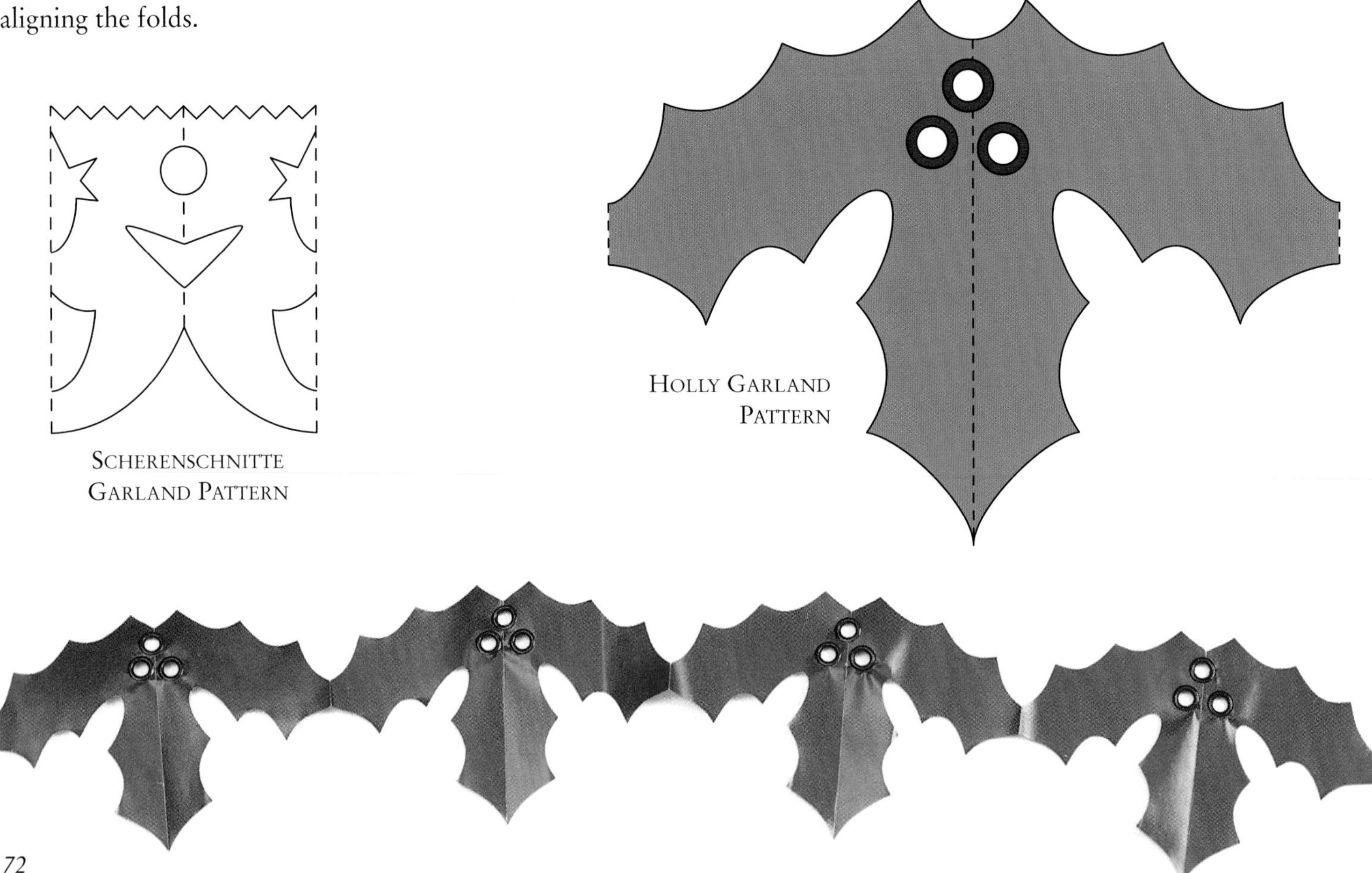

SCHERENSCHNITTE GARLAND PATTERN

HOLLY GARLAND PATTERN

Scherenschnitte, the Pennsylvania German folk craft of ornate scissor-cutting, makes a delightful tree trim. These garlands are made from paper and eyelets or tea-dyed felt.

Scissor-Cut Garlands

Cookie Cutter Snowmen

Use air-dry clay to create a family of smiling snowpeople. Beads, buttons, and snippets of ribbon are colorful finishing accents.

What You'll Need

Drill; ⅛-inch bit
Copper cookie cutter in gingerbread man or snowman shape
File; heavy copper wire
Wire cutter
Needle-nose pliers
Orange oven-bake clay, such as Sculpey
White air-dry clay, such as Crayola Model Magic
Crafts knife
Large black seed beads; toothpicks
Assorted small buttons
Thick white crafts glue
Paint-on glitter medium
Paintbrush
⅛- to ⅜-inch-wide ribbon
Scissors

What To Do

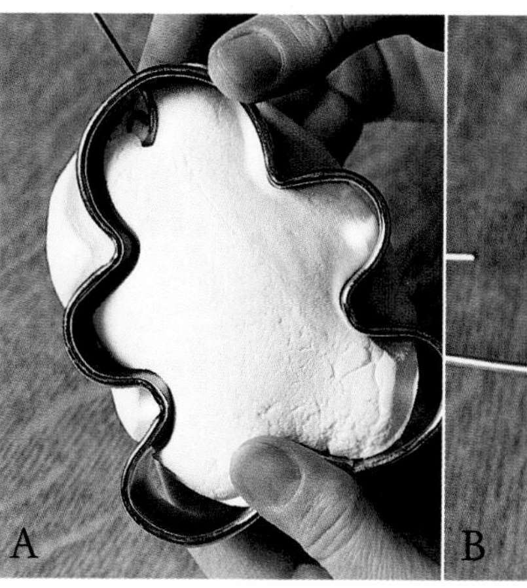
A

B

1 Drill a small hole in the top center of the cookie cutter. Smooth any sharp edges with a file, being careful not to mar the surface of the cookie cutter. Cut a 6-inch-long piece of wire. Make a loop at one end. Push straight end through hole in cookie cutter. Shape wire into a hanger.

2 Break a toothpick in half. Shape a ½-inch-long carrot nose from orange clay. Press broken toothpick into the center of the wide end of carrot shape to secure. Bake in the oven according to the manufacturer's directions. Let cool.

3 Shape a ball of white clay about the size of an orange. Flatten slightly.

4 From the back side of the cookie cutter, press clay into the cutter, letting it bulge slightly on the front side as shown in Photo A, *above right*. Fill space in cutter with clay. Trim excess clay away, leaving the back side flush with the cookie cutter.

5 Using a toothpick, poke holes into the clay as guides for the eyes, nose, and mouth. Using a toothpick, gently press seed beads into the poked holes for the eyes and mouth as shown in Photo B. Place beads on sideways to conceal their holes. Push the toothpick attached to the carrot nose into the clay. Press buttons in place. Let dry.

6 If necessary, use crafts glue to reattach any buttons or beads that may have fallen off during drying.

7 Paint the front of the snowman with glitter medium. Let dry.

8 Tie a ribbon scarf around the cookie cutter snowman. Trim the ribbon ends as needed.

Santa's Li'l Helpers

With milkweed pod ears and paper hats, these whimsical elves bring a touch of humor to evergreen branches.

WHAT YOU'LL NEED

Scraper or abrasive scrubbing pad
Small dried ornamental gourds
Soapy water
Sharp non-serrated knife
Milkweed pods; wood stain; rag
Hot-glue gun; hot-glue sticks
Pencil; coral color pencil
Fine permanent black marker
Thick white crafts glue; allspice
Tracing paper; scissors
Decorative paper; double-stick tape
Ribbon; wood stars

WHAT TO DO

1 Scrape and clean dried ornamental gourds using warm soapy water and a scraper or scrubbing pad. Use a knife on tough spots if necessary. Wipe dry.

2 Clean debris from inside of milkweed pods.

3 Use a rag to apply wood stain to gourd and inside of milkweed pods. Wipe and let dry.

4 Pencil in eyes, nose, and mouth. Lightly color two small cheek circles using a coral color pencil. Draw mouth and eyebrows with a black permanent marker. Use glue to attach pieces, including allspice for eyes and nose.

5 Enlarge and trace hat patterns, *below*, onto tracing paper, cut out, and trace onto decorative paper. Cut out and use double-stick tape to hold together.

6 Insert a length of ribbon loop through tip of hat for hanging. Hot-glue pinecone, star, or pistachio shell on tip of hat.

7 Glue the hat onto the head. Let dry.

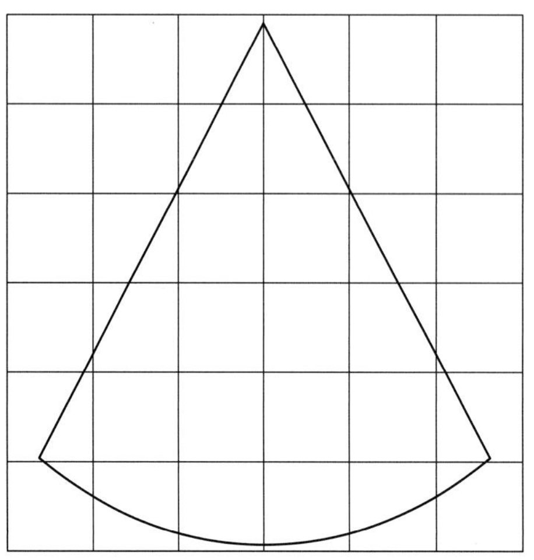

TALL ELF HAT PATTERN 1 SQUARE = 1 INCH

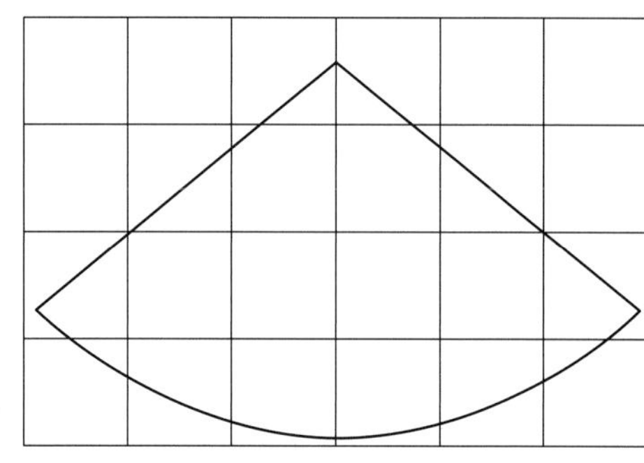

SHORT ELF HAT PATTERN 1 SQUARE = 1 INCH

Confetti Celebration

Instead of sprinkling confetti into a card or onto a tabletop, let it bring cheer to an ordinary round sphere. Pick any shape of confetti to enhance a plain ornament.

WHAT YOU'LL NEED

Matte-finish ornament
Large spiral confetti
Thick white crafts glue
Cup to hold ornament; cord

WHAT TO DO

1 Working on one side at a time, glue confetti randomly to the ornament. Place in cup and let dry. Rotate the ornament and glue confetti to the remaining side. Let dry. Add a piece of cord for hanger.

Candy Strands

WHAT YOU'LL NEED

Colorful candy, such as sour-apple candy rings, saltwater taffy, and jelly candy
White cord
White dental floss
Needle
Hot-glue gun; glue sticks

WHAT TO DO

1 For the sour-apple candy ring garland, loop and link candy together with cord to the desired garland length.

2 For the jelly candy garland, thread a needle with dental floss. String the candies on the floss.

3 For the taffy garland, connect the twisted wrapper ends with a dot of hot glue. Let cool.

Look for the juiciest colors of your favorite candies to make eye-catching garlands.

Make that plain-Jane ornament seem special with a coat of colorful nail polish painted in fancy swirls and stripes.

Polished Ornaments

WHAT YOU'LL NEED

Newspapers
Matte- or shiny-finish ornament
Plain or glitter fingernail polish
Pipe cleaner

WHAT TO DO

1 In a well-ventilated work area, cover work surface with newspapers. Holding the ornament by the hanger, use the brush in the fingernail polish to paint the ornament with stripes, dots, swirls, or other designs. The polish may pull off some of the original color of the ornament, revealing the silver beneath. Hang the ornament from a pipe cleaner ring to dry.

2 For a snow-capped ornament, paint the top two-thirds with white glitter fingernail polish. Let dry.

Cleverly Candied

Kids will have a jolly good time transforming picnicware into whimsical trims. Made to resemble candies, these don't-eat sweets are crafted from clay. Turn the page for the full assortment.

What You'll Need

FOR ALL ORNAMENTS

Woodburning tool; paintbrush
Air-dry clay, such as Crayola Model Magic
⅛-inch-wide ribbon or thread

FOR THE ORANGE FORK/GUMDROP

Orange plastic fork
Acrylic paints in white, red, yellow, and green
Decoupage medium; coarse salt

FOR THE RED FORK/GREEN CANDY

Red plastic fork
Gold glitter paint
Couscous pasta
White opaque acrylic texture gel
Acrylic paint in green and light green
Gold candy sprinkles

FOR THE GREEN FORK/PINK HEART

Green plastic fork
Gold glitter paint
Green sequins
Candy sprinkles
Acrylic paint in pink, green, and red
White opaque acrylic texturizing gel

FOR THE PINK SPOON/ CANDY-COATED CHOCOLATE DOTS

Pink plastic spoon
Thick white crafts glue

FOR THE YELLOW SPOON/ PEPPERMINT

Yellow plastic spoon
Acrylic paints in red, blue, and green; fine liner brush
Couscous pasta
Opaque white acrylic texturizing gel
Toothpick

FOR THE GREEN SPOON/CHERRY

Green plastic spoon
White opaque texturizing acrylic gel
Toothpick; artificial cherry

What To Do

1 Use a woodburning tool to melt a hole in the handle end of each piece to use for hanging.

FOR THE GUMDROP FORK

1 For fork handle, dip handle end of paintbrush in white paint and dot on a row of white dots. Let dry.

2 Roll gumdrop shapes from clay. While clay is soft, press shapes together side by side and quickly paint red, yellow, and green. Press painted gumdrops onto fork tines before drying entirely. Touch up paint if needed.

3 Paint gumdrops with decoupage medium and sprinkle with coarse salt. Let dry.

4 Thread a 10-inch length of ribbon through hole in handle. Tie into a bow. Tie on a thread hanger.

FOR THE RED FORK/GREEN CANDY

1 Paint dots onto fork handle using gold glitter paint. Let dry. Paint couscous green. Let dry.

Instructions are continued on pages 84–85.

2 Shape square from clay, making the corners rounded and about ⅝ inch thick. Work quickly and do not allow it to dry.

3 Mix pastel green paint into acrylic texture gel and paint generously onto clay square as if spreading frosting, leaving bottom portion unpainted.

4 Press the candy piece into the fork tines and touch up paint as needed.

5 Press green painted couscous and gold candies into green. Let dry.

6 Tie on a ribbon and a thread hanger.

FOR THE GREEN FORK/PINK HEART

1 Paint red stripes on the handle. Let dry. Dot a generous amount of gold glitter paint onto red stripes and press green sequins into gold glitter. Let dry.

2 Paint candy sprinkles red and green. Let dry.

3 Shape a heart from clay, about ⅝ inch thick. Mix a small dab of pink paint into gel and paint thickly onto heart shape, leaving bottom portion unpainted. Press heart shape onto tines of fork and touch up paint as needed.

4 Press green and red candy sprinkles into pink. Let dry. Tie on a ribbon and hanger.

FOR THE PINK SPOON/ CANDY-COATED CHOCOLATE DOTS

1 Shape candies from clay. Let dry.

2 Paint candies different colors. Let dry. Glue onto spoon. Let dry. Tie on a ribbon and hanger.

FOR THE YELLOW SPOON/ PEPPERMINT

1 Shape peppermint from clay. Let dry.

2 Paint red stripes on peppermint. Let dry. Paint a few pieces of couscous blue and green. Let dry.

3 Place white texturizing gel onto spoon and swirl with a toothpick. Insert peppermint and press on couscous. Let dry. Tie on a ribbon and hanger.

FOR THE GREEN SPOON/CHERRY

1 Place gel onto spoon and swirl a toothpick through it. Insert cherry. Let dry.

2 Tie on a ribbon and thread hanger.

NOTE: *Be sure children know these are not for eating.*

Fun & Fancy

Wonderland Icicles

WHAT YOU'LL NEED

20-gauge wire; ruler; wire cutters
7mm and 9mm clear plastic beads
Assorted silver sequins and mirror sequin discs
Needle-nose pliers; ribbon or thread

WHAT TO DO

1 Cut a 24-inch length of wire. String about 7 inches of 9mm beads onto the wire, inserting sequins and mirror sequin discs randomly. Above and below the length of 9mm beads, string 4 inches of the 7mm beads, sequins, and discs randomly.

2 Bring both ends of the wire together to form a loop, and thread 2 inches of 9mm beads and sequins onto the combined wires. String 1 inch of the 7mm beads onto the wire. Attach one sequin or mirror sequin disc to the end of the wires. Using the pliers, coil the remaining wire into a knot to hold beads in place. Trim any excess wire. Twist the loop to form a long, narrow icicle. Hang on the tree with ribbon or thread, or loop it over a branch.

Tulle-Filled Trims

(shown opposite)

WHAT YOU'LL NEED

Tulle: scrap of green, pink, blue, or lavender
Ruler; scissors
Small metallic sequins in various colors and shapes
Hot-glue gun; hot-glue sticks
Clear glass ball ornament with removable topper
Pencil

WHAT TO DO

1 Measure and cut a 4-inch square of tulle. Glue six to eight sequins to tulle square in a random pattern.

2 Remove the topper from the ornament. Insert the tulle using the pencil to push it inside. Replace the topper.

Silver Stars

(shown opposite)

WHAT YOU'LL NEED

Cutting mat (or folded newspaper, cardboard, or magazine)

36-gauge aluminum tooling foil (available at crafts stores)
Ruler; pencil
Scissors; tin punch; silver thread

WHAT TO DO

1 Using the cutting mat as a pad, draw a star shape on the foil using the pencil and ruler. Cut out the star.

2 Draw designs on the star with the pencil, pressing firmly to indent the foil.

3 Use a tin punch to make a hole at the top of star. Tie a thread through the holes for a hanger.

Beaded icicles, tulle-filled spheres, and silver stars combine with coordinating trims for a festive tree your family and friends will remember forever.

An Unexpected Twist

Step aside, traditional trims! Here comes a treeful of ornaments loaded with wonder and whimsy. We've combined some unusual colors, very unique crafting supplies, and newly discovered ways of using familiar materials to create this ever-so-fun array of Christmas ornaments and garlands.

Painted Tile Trio

Head for the hardware store to gather tiny tiles and plumbing flanges to make this contemporary trio of holiday ornaments.

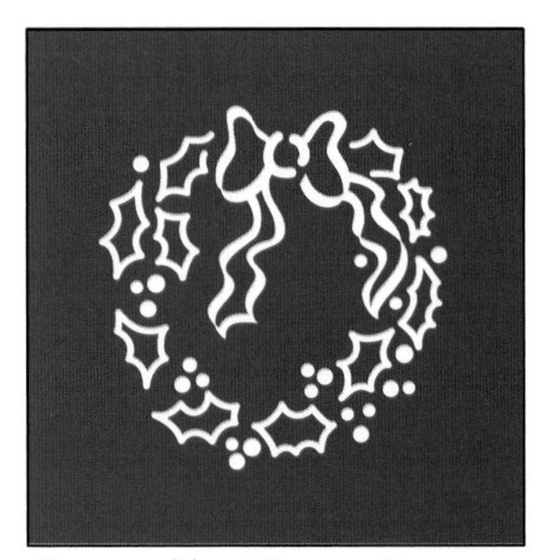
Painted Tile Wreath Pattern

Painted Tile Snowman Pattern

What You'll Need

Drill with fine bit
Metal flange for ⅜-inch iron pipe or ½-inch copper tube (available in hardware stores and home centers)
Heavy crafts wire; wire cutter
Needle-nose pliers
Fine-tip paintbrush
2-inch ceramic tile in white, red, or green (available in home centers)
Strong adhesive, such as E6000
Pencil; cardboard
Felt to match tile; transfer paper
Acrylic glass paints in black or white

Painted Tile Tree Pattern

What To Do

1 Drill a hole in the edge of the flange. Cut a 6-inch piece of wire. Wrap wire around a paintbrush to coil. Insert one end of wire through hole in flange. Using needle-nose pliers, form a tiny loop at the end of the wire to secure it in the flange. Shape the wire as desired for the ornament hanger.

2 Wash and dry the tile. Glue it inside the flange. Let the glue dry.

3 Trace around the flange on cardboard and again on felt. Cut the cardboard piece slightly smaller than drawn circle. Cut the felt slightly larger than drawn circle. Glue the cardboard on the back of the tile. Glue the felt on the cardboard. Let dry.

4 Trace the desired pattern, *left*. Transfer the design to the tile. Paint over the pattern lines using white on red and green tiles and black on white tiles. Let dry.

All-American Evergreen

Show your love of country with red, white, and blue cocarde ornaments, a striking star tree topper, and a star-studded felt and bead garland.

Instructions are on pages 94–95.

All-American Evergreen *continued*

WHAT YOU'LL NEED
FOR THE PATRIOTIC COCARDE ORNAMENT

2 yards of 1½-inch-wide grosgrain ribbon
Thread; needle
Two decorative buttons
Cord

WHAT TO DO
FOR THE PATRIOTIC COCARDE ORNAMENT

1 Baste under ¼ inch at one end of ribbon as shown in Diagram A, *opposite*. Fold the end of ribbon at a right angle, matching fold to selvage. Finger-press as shown in Diagram B.

2 Fold ribbon as shown in Diagram C. Hand-tack at top to make first point.

3 Fold ribbon at a right angle again as shown in Diagram D; finger-press. Align this triangle with the first triangle and hand-tack top points together.

4 Repeat step 3 to make 20 points, referring to Diagrams E and F as guides. Continue folding half a point, trimming and turning under ¼ inch at end of ribbon. Hand-stitch end to beginning to make 21 points.

5 Sew a decorative button in the center of the cocarde on both sides. Add a cord hanger.

WHAT YOU'LL NEED
FOR THE STAR-SPANGLED TOPPER

3 yards of 2⅛-inch-wide grosgrain ribbon
12-inch square of blue felt
12-inch square of white felt
Fusible web
Blue thread; pinking shears
Fabric glue
Five star appliqués
½-inch satin ribbon

WHAT TO DO
FOR THE STAR-SPANGLED TOPPER

1 Make a 21-point cocarde from 2⅛-inch-wide ribbon following Step 1 through Step 4 as for the Patriotic Cocarde, *left*.

2 Trace the star pattern, *page 96.* Cut out the pattern. Use the pattern to cut out a blue star. Fuse the star to white felt. Machine-stitch around blue star close to edge.

3 Using a pinking shears, trim ¼ inch beyond the blue star.

4 Secure the center of the cocarde to the center of the felt star with a decorative button. Glue the back of the cocarde to the star. Glue star appliqués to the points of the felt star.

5 Tie a generous satin ribbon bow and tack it to the bottom of the cocarde.

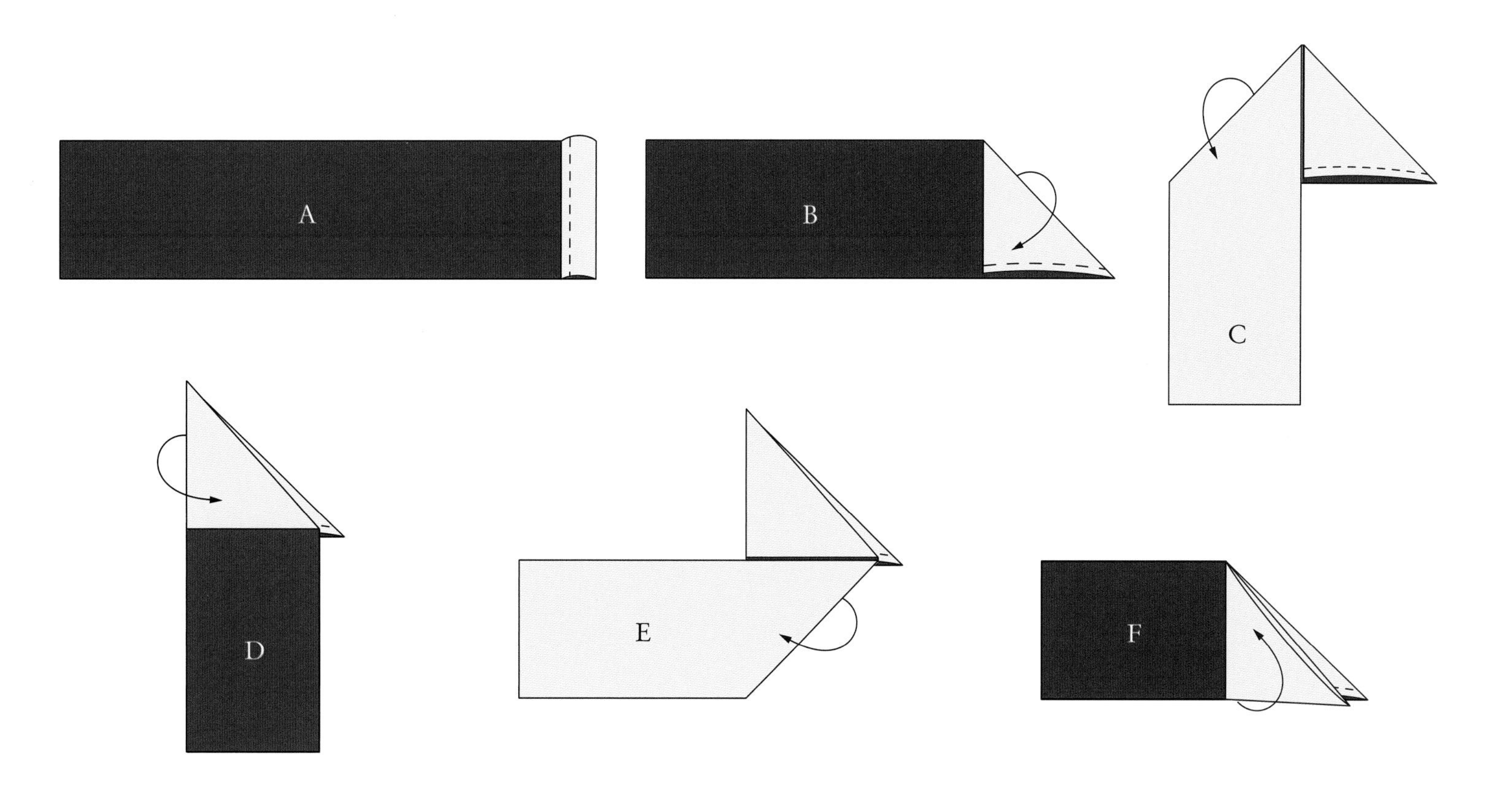

What You'll Need
for the Pride Garland

Tracing paper
Pencil
Blue felt
Scissors
15mm white beads
13mm red beads
#3 or #5 pearl cotton
Needle

What To Do
for the Pride Garland

1 Trace the star pattern, *page 96.* Cut out. Trace around the star pattern as many times as desired for garland. Cut stars from blue felt.

2 Thread needle with pearl cotton. Knot one end. Poke needle through center of one felt star. Alternately thread red and white beads to the desired garland length. For garlands longer than 36 inches, tie garland lengths together.

Patterns on page 96.

All-American Evergreen *continued*

Pride Garland
Star Pattern

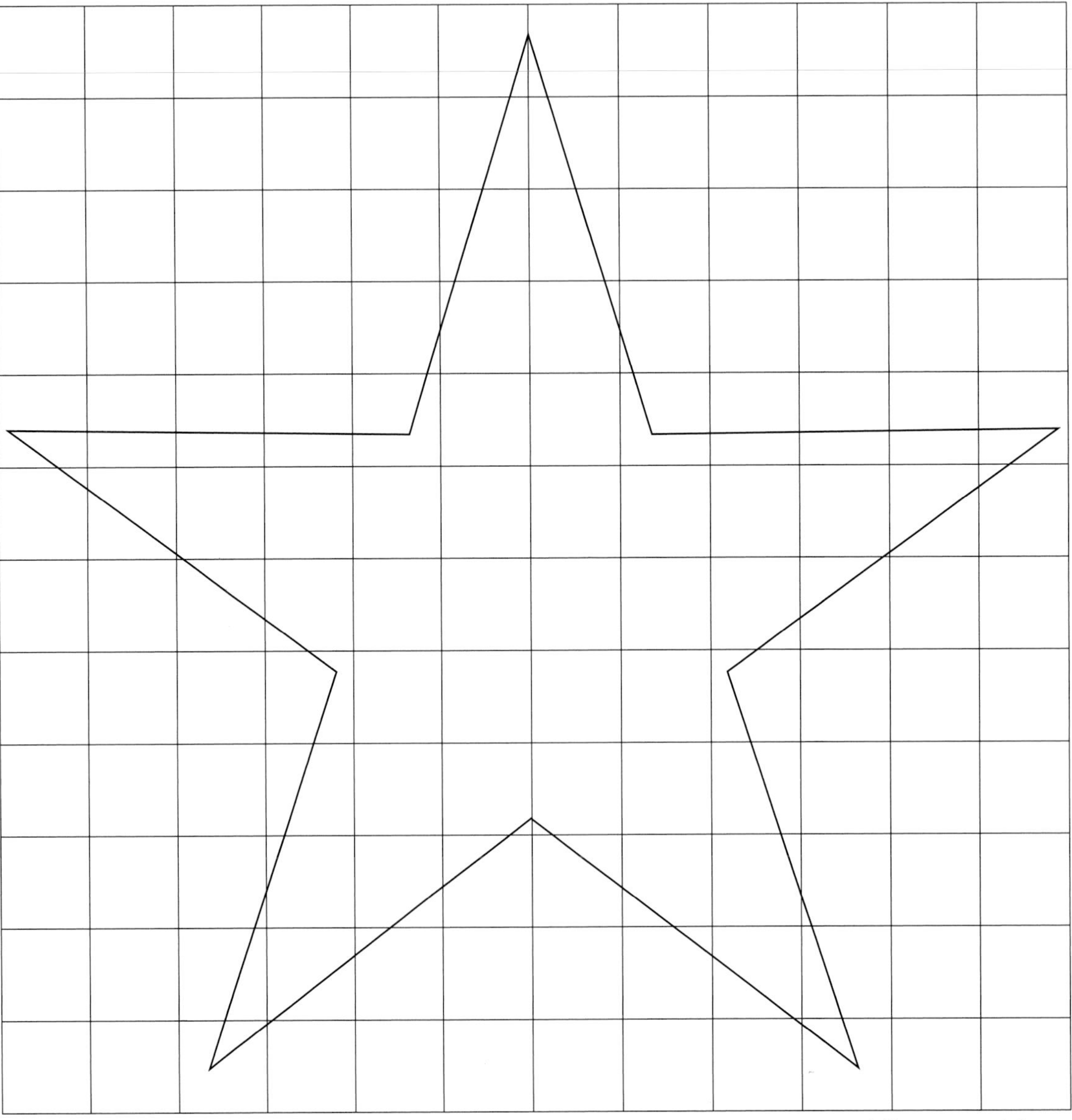

Star-Spangled Topper Pattern 1 Square = 1 Inch

Jingle Link

Whether you choose gold, silver, or other colors of bells, this holiday garland will jingle all the way. For variety, add beads or buttons to the musical trim.

WHAT YOU'LL NEED

Gold, silver, or colored medium-weight wire
Wire cutter; jingle bells
Pencil
Miniature Christmas tree light trims

WHAT TO DO

1 Cut off desired length of wire for the garland. String on jingle bells and lights, spacing approximately 6 inches apart. Twist the wire once to secure each bell and light in place.

2 Between each trim, wrap the wire around a pencil to spiral the wire. Remove pencil. Shape the wire as desired.

Kitchen Creations

Transform shapely kitchen tools into colorful trims for the tree with metallic paint and a sprinkling of glitter.

WHAT YOU'LL NEED

Awl
Lemon reamer, honey dipper, or other wood kitchen tool
Small eye screws
Metallic paints in blue, gold, green, pink, purple, and silver
Paintbrush
Decoupage medium
Iridescent white glitter
Sheer ribbon
Scissors

WHAT TO DO

1 Use an awl to poke a hole in the end of the reamer or other handle. Twist eye screws into the holes.

2 Paint the tool gold. Let dry. Using the sections of the wood pieces as guides, paint each section a different color of metallic paint, allowing the gold to show through. Paint alternating color stripes on the handle of the honey dipper. Let dry. Highlight the painted areas with the metallic paints as desired. Let dry.

3 Apply dots with the handle end of a paintbrush and paint as desired. Let dry.

4 Coat utensils with decoupage medium. Sprinkle glitter on the wet areas. Let dry. Shake off excess glitter.

5 Thread ribbon through eye screw. Tie into a bow. Trim ribbon ends.

Magnificent Marbles

Beautifully striated with pure, deep color or clear with sparkles and flecks, glass shooters and standard-size marbles make prized ornaments.

WHAT YOU'LL NEED
Wire cutters
Heavy wire
Needle-nose pliers
Dowel
Marbles

WHAT TO DO

1 Cut 14-inch lengths of wire. Using pliers, curl one end of wire. Wrap wire around a dowel. Remove dowel.

2 Hold marble at the top of the coil and continue winding wire, securing marble in place. Coil wire as desired.

3 Use pliers to shape the top of the remaining wire into a hanging loop.

Leaf-Laden

WHAT YOU'LL NEED

Drill and small drill bit
Wood ball
Eye screw
Rubber cement
Leaf or fern
Dye in desired color, such as Rit
¼-inch-wide ribbon

WHAT TO DO

1 Drill a hole in the wood ball. Twist the eye screw into the hole until secure.

2 Apply rubber cement to one side of the leaf or fern. Place the cement side onto the wood ball. Press the edges firmly to adhere to the ball.

3 Dip the ball in dye. Remove from dye. Let the ball dry. Remove the leaf or fern. Thread a 10-inch length of ribbon through the eye screw. Knot the ribbon ends, leaving 1 inch at each ribbon end. Slide the knotted end of the ribbon next to the eye screw.

Capture the silhouette of a favorite leaf or fern with these earthy, dyed wooden ball ornaments.

Silvery Sensations

Make a few additions to your hardware shopping list to create these contemporary trims. A garland of painted chain completes the tinseled tree.

WHAT YOU'LL NEED
FOR THE CHAIN GARLAND

Newspapers
Chain in desired pattern
Metallic spray paint

WHAT TO DO
FOR THE CHAIN GARLAND

1 In a well-ventilated work area, cover work surface with newspapers. Spray-paint the chain. Let dry. Turn it over and repeat.

WHAT YOU'LL NEED
FOR THE METALLIC SNOWFLAKES

Scissors
Metallic embroidery ribbon in magenta or turquoise
Large-eyed needle
3⅙-inch aluminum drain guard (available at hardware stores and home centers)

WHAT TO DO
FOR THE METALLIC SNOWFLAKES

1 Cut a 30-inch-long piece of embroidery ribbon. Make a large knot in one end. Thread the ribbon on a needle.

2 If the drain guard has tabs on the back, break them off.

3 From the back, bring the needle through the center hole in the drain guard. Following the stitching diagrams, *below,* stitch a snowflake design. Secure the ribbon ends on the back.

4 Cut a 7-inch piece of ribbon for the hanger. Thread it through one of the outer holes. Knot the ends together.

WHAT YOU'LL NEED
FOR THE SILVER DROPS

Small silver ball ornaments; pencil
Strong adhesive, such as E6000
Cake decorating tip; wire cutter
Fine colored metallic crafts wire

WHAT TO DO
FOR THE SILVER DROPS

1 Remove the ornament topper. Glue topper end of ornament into cake decorating tip. Let dry.

2 Cut an 18-inch length of wire. Wrap a third of the wire around the handle of a pencil to coil. Remove pencil. Continue by winding the wire up and around the ornament. Loop remaining wire in half; twist to secure, leaving a loop for hanging.

STITCHING DIAGRAMS

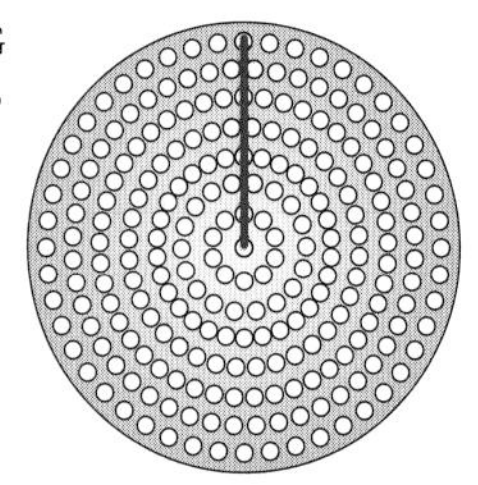
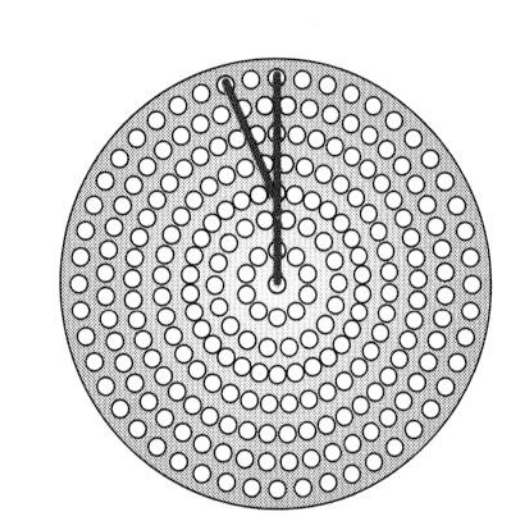
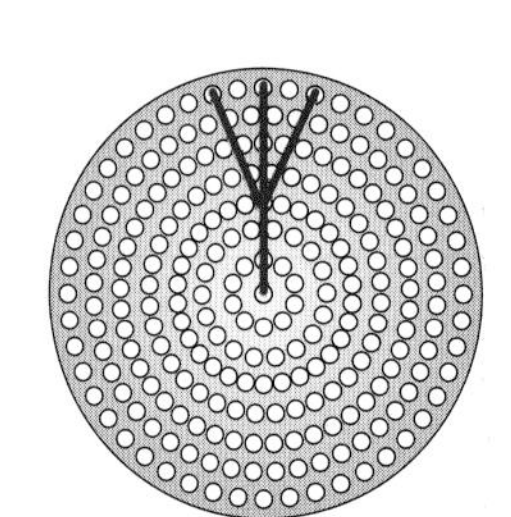

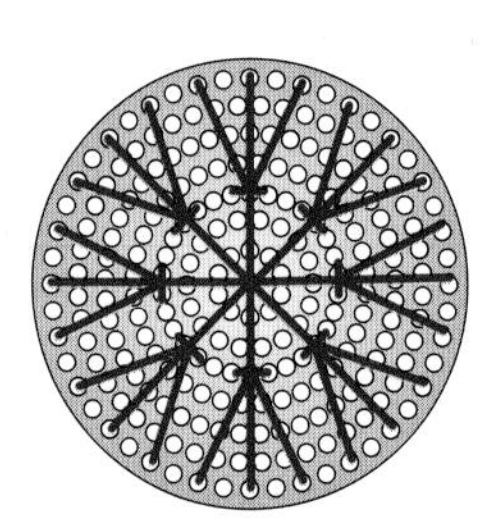

Wintry Walnuts

Natural and manufactured textures combine in this pastel, glistening, pretty-as-a-sugarplum holiday ornament.

WHAT YOU'LL NEED

Newspapers
English walnuts
White spray primer
Metallic and iridescent acrylic paints in baby blue, lavender, pale green, pink, white, and yellow
Paintbrush
Small gold eye screws
White glue; white glitter
Tracing paper; pencil
Scissors
Textured paper; paper punch
¼- and 1-inch-wide pastel sheer wired ribbon

WHAT TO DO

1 In a well-ventilated work area, cover work surface with newspapers. Spray walnuts with white spray primer. Let dry.

2 Paint walnuts using a combination of two colors, painting half of the walnut one color and the other half a second color. Blend the two colors together where they meet before the paint dries. Let dry.

3 Gently screw in a small eye screw at one end of the walnut.

4 Thin white glue with a few drops of water. Paint the thinned glue onto the painted walnut. While wet, sprinkle white glitter on the walnut. Let dry.

5 Trace the leaf pattern, *below left,* onto tracing paper. Cut out the patterns and trace around them on textured paper (one for each walnut). Cut out the leaves. Paint the leaves pale green. Let dry. Paint on a thinned coat of glue. While wet, sprinkle with glitter. Let dry. Punch a hole in the center of each leaf.

6 Thread an 8-inch length of ¼-inch-wide ribbon through eye screw. Tie a generous ribbon bow through the eye screw. Knot the ends. Tie a wide ribbon bow around narrow ribbon, if desired.

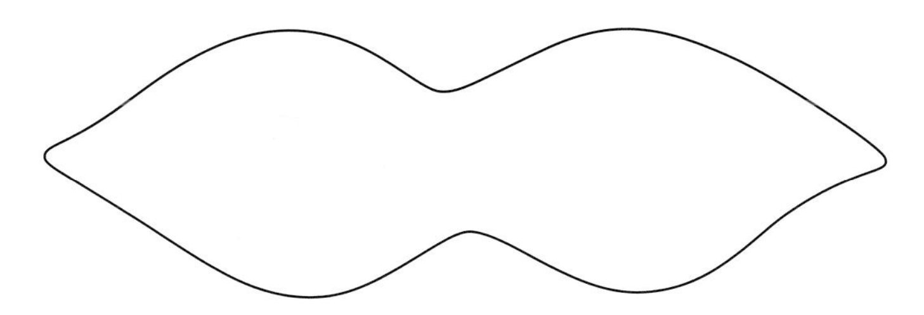

LEAF PATTERN

What You'll Need

Two 10-inch-square coordinating papers for each envelope
Spray adhesive; tracing paper
Pencil; scissors
Ruler; utility knife
Paper punch
Thick white crafts glue
Cording to coordinate with papers
8-inch-long piece of fine crafts wire
Seed and other small beads
Star bead

Envelope Pattern   1 Square = 1 Inch

What To Do

1 Spray adhesive on the back of each piece of paper. Carefully place the glued sides together, avoiding wrinkles.

2 Enlarge and trace the pattern, *left*, onto tracing paper. Cut out and trace onto prepared decorative paper. Cut out.

3 To make crisp folds, refer to dotted lines on pattern and use a ruler. Place ruler on fold line on the inside of paper. Lightly score along the lines with utility knife. Fold over the flaps.

4 Punch a hanging hole in the tip of the ornament.

5 Draw a line of white glue around edge of paper. Apply cording trim. Let dry.

6 Use glue to secure the folded flaps. Glue decorative bead where paper ends overlap.

7 Poke wire through top of ornament. Thread assorted beads onto each end of wire, securing the end beads. Shape wire into a hanger.

Elegant Envelopes

Create a folded paper envelope that's the right size to cradle a gift certificate or a little holiday green.

What You'll Need

Matte-finish ornament
Large sequin spangles in assorted colors (available at crafts stores)
Thick white crafts glue
Cup to hold ornament

What To Do

1 Working on one side at a time, glue sequins randomly to the ornament. Set it in a cup and let dry. Rotate the ornament and glue sequins to the remaining side. Let dry.

Sequin Studded

An unusual color combination for a traditional holiday— these oversize sequins make a contemporary statement on this rich purple ornament. The metallic checkerboard surface of the trims reflects light like a hologram.

Ribbon Candy

WHAT YOU'LL NEED

22 inches of wired or unwired ribbon in desired width
Needle
Thread
Assorted beads and buttons

WHAT TO DO

1 Thread needle and knot thread ends together. Push needle through one end of ribbon. Form first ribbon loop by pushing needle through ribbon a few inches from first spot. Form ribbon loops by stitching through the center of each loop and threading the needle through a bead or several beads between each loop.

2 When the ornament is complete, add a hanging loop of ribbon or threaded beads to the top. If desired, add a beaded dangle or a ribbon streamer at the bottom, sewing through a button placed beneath the ribbon for stability.

Ribbon loops tacked together with tiny stitches mimic holiday candies. The delicate beads that separate the layers add a hint of elegance to these quick-stitch ornaments.

Message in a Bottle

These bottles won't be found floating onto shore, but they are sure to bring good fortune to all those who receive one.

WHAT YOU'LL NEED

Small bottle with lid
Glass paints
Acrylic paint
Paintbrush
Red parchment paper
Decorative scissors
Black and gold fine permanent markers
Small piece of Christmas tinsel garland
Colored plastic-coated wire

WHAT TO DO

1 Wash and dry the bottle. Following the manufacturer's directions, paint tiny designs around the top of the bottle with glass paints. Choose simple motifs such as holly, candy canes, or bells. Let the paint dry. Bake if required by the manufacturer's instructions.

2 Paint the lid with acrylic paint. Let dry.

3 Cut a note-size paper from the parchment using the decorative scissors. Write a message on the note. Decorate the note, if desired, with the gold marker.

4 Place the garland in the bottle. Roll the note into a tube and put in the bottle. Screw on the lid. Wrap the wire around the neck of the bottle and form a loop for hanging.

MESSAGE IDEAS

- *I love you! Meet me for lunch on December 24th—my treat!*
- *You will receive a free car wash from Dad!*
- *May your holidays be blessed with family and friends.*
- *Let your heart be filled with Christmas joy.*
- *Take time to enjoy the season's magic.*
- *Here are three hours of babysitting for you from me!*
- *Merry Christmas! Look under the chair for your gift.*
- *I'll do dishes for you for a whole week! Your kid!*

Metal Magic

Simple materials from the hardware store can make surprisingly striking garlands. The metal and glass reflect the color and sparkle of the season.

WHAT YOU'LL NEED
FOR THE METAL GARLANDS
(shown opposite)

Turnbuckles
¼×2-inch flathead machine screws with nuts
⅛-inch quick-link bolts
3/16×3-inch eyebolts with nuts
Antique keys
Silver ribbon
Beads
Needle-nose pliers
Soldering wire

WHAT TO DO
FOR THE METAL GARLANDS

1 For the nuts-and-bolts strand, link turnbuckles, machine screws, quick-link bolts, and eyebolts.

2 For the key garland, tie keys onto silver ribbon, leaving approximately 2 inches between keys.

3 For the wire garland, use needle-nose pliers to shape wire into curves that link at the ends, adding beads along the way.

WHAT YOU'LL NEED
FOR THE GLASS GARLANDS

Glass cubes (available in floral supply stores)
White tulle
Crystal teardrops and prisms
Beaded extension chain (available in the lighting section of the hardware store)
French jewelry pins (2¼-inch no-coil safety pins)
15-watt clear-flame or bent-tip lightbulbs

WHAT TO DO
FOR THE GLASS GARLANDS

1 For the cubes garland, form a tube from tulle. Knot at one end. Wrap a glass cube next to the knot and tie another knot on the other side. Repeat to complete the entire length of garland.

2 For the teardrop chain, string prisms and crystal teardrops along a beaded extension chain.

3 For the bulb garland, link jewelry pins end to end, attaching lightbulbs to every other pin.

Happy Holiday Motifs

The joyous symbols of the season are lovingly reflected in this chapter of smile-provoking ornaments. From sculpted St. Nicks to fancy stitched holiday stockings, you'll find ornaments to give and to treasure.

Pretty Pair

Chenille yarn and velour trims wrap these heart and pear papier-mâché shapes with rich softness. Metallic accents give these red and green ornaments a polished finish.

Instructions are on page 118.

Pretty Pair *continued*

WHAT YOU'LL NEED

Papier-mâché or plastic foam base in desired shape
Thick white crafts glue
Assorted chenille yarn or velour trim
Scissors
Star-shape tacks
Round upholstery tacks
Gold cord
Gold braid
⅛-inch-wide gold ribbon
Straight pin
Gold silk leaf

WHAT TO DO

1 Work on one section of the papier-mâché or plastic foam shape at a time. Cover a small section with glue and wind yarn or trim around (or form it to) the shape, until completely covered. Complete each section to cover the entire shape. Let the glue dry.

2 For the heart, use glue to draw a symmetrical design onto the yarn- or trim-covered front. Gently press cording into the glue. Glue gold braid around the edge of the heart. Let the glue dry. Add brass tacks on the cord design as shown in the photograph on *page 116.*

3 For the pear, press two or more star-shape tacks into the pear where desired.

4 For each ornament, cut a 6-inch length of ribbon for hanging. Glue and pin in place, adding a gold silk leaf to the pear. Let the glue dry.

This freehand star, crafted from a thin sheet of copper, looks heavenly on a Christmas tree. Eyelets add a touch of gold to the star points.

Shiny Copper Star

WHAT YOU'LL NEED

Pencil
Tracing paper; scissors
Nickel
Thin sheet of copper
Tin snips
Work gloves
Paper punch
Gold eyelets and eyelet tool
Towel; gold cord

WHAT TO DO

1 Draw a free-form star, approximately 5 inches high, on tracing paper. Use a nickel as a guide to draw circular shapes on each star point. Cut out.

2 Trace around the pattern on a sheet of copper. Wearing gloves, cut out. Punch a hole in the center of the circle on each star point. Secure an eyelet in each hole.

3 From the right side of the ornament, use a pencil to trace the star shape into the copper ¼ inch from the edge, extending the lines to the center of the star as shown, *above.* Turn the ornament over on a towel. Use a pencil to color in between the drawn lines to add dimension to the ornament. Thread cord through one eyelet to hang.

Charming St. Nick

Curls of clay make this Santa seem happy from the top of his hat to the tip of his beard. Use oven-bake clay to create this clever fellow.

What You'll Need

Oven-bake clay, such as Sculpey, in beige, white, dark red, green, and black
Glass baking dish with flat bottom
Paper clip
¼-inch-wide ribbon
Scissors

What To Do

1 Make a golf ball-size piece of beige clay. Shape into an oval and flatten until the shape is approximately ½-inch thick. Place the oval in the center of the baking dish.

2 For nose, roll two pea-size beige balls and one slightly larger ball. Press a smaller ball on each side of the larger one. Press the nose in the center of the oval.

3 Make half a golf ball-size piece of red clay. Shape into a ½-inch-thick triangle. Pull and shape one triangle point to form the hat's tip. Bend the tip slightly to the left. Place the hat on one end of the oval and press together.

4 For the hat brim, roll a piece of white clay into a 3-inch-long cylinder, approximately the diameter of a pencil. Roll the ends into points. Shape the piece into an arch. Shape each end into a small coil. Press the shape firmly over the area where the hat meets the oval.

5 Make a large white coil for the tip of the hat. Make small white coils for the beard, mustache, and eyebrows, noting the shapes for each in the photograph, *opposite*. Make three small green coils for the hat embellishments. Press coils in place.

6 For eyes, roll two tiny black ovals. Press into place just above the nose.

7 Bend a U-shape piece from a paper clip. Push the ends into the top of the hat, leaving a small loop for the hanger.

8 Bake the ornament in the oven according to the clay manufacturer's instructions. Let cool. Thread an 8-inch piece of ribbon through the paper clip loop. Tie the ribbon ends into a bow. Trim the ribbon ends.

Hand-Stitched Stockings

Use scraps of felt to create these miniature stockings for St. Nick. Cotton embroidery floss is used for the simple stitches that accent holly, Santa's initial, and floral motifs.

Instructions are on page 124.

Hand-Stitched Stockings *continued*

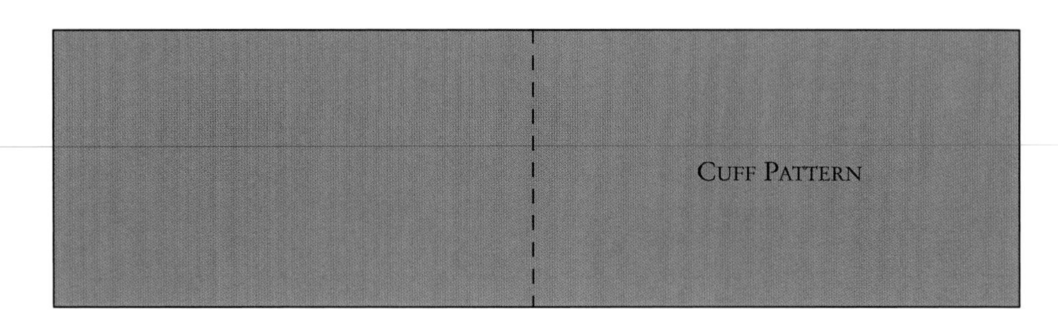

CUFF PATTERN

WHAT YOU'LL NEED

Tracing paper
Pencil
Scissors
Felt scraps
Embroidery floss in coordinating colors
Needle

WHAT TO DO

1 Trace the stocking and desired stocking front design onto tracing paper. Cut out the patterns. Use the patterns to cut the pieces from felt.

2 Using the patterns as guides, sew the felt motifs on the stocking front using embroidery floss and running stitches, whipstitches, or French knots. For the floral motif, stitch lazy daisy leaves. Make French knot accents on the initial and holly stockings.

3 Align a front and back stocking. Using floss and blanket stitches, sew the front to the back. Align the short ends of the cuff. Stitch the ends together using blanket stitches. Work blanket stitches around the bottom edge of the cuff, joining it to the top of the stocking, sewing through only one layer of the stocking. Work blanket stitches around the top edge of the cuff.

4 Cut a 2×¼-inch hanger, per pattern. Fold the felt piece in half, short ends together. Tuck the ends inside the stocking cuff on the heel side. Use embroidery floss and a cross-stitch to secure the hanger.

HANGER PATTERN

HOLLY PATTERN

FLOWER PATTERN

INITIAL STOCKING PLACEMENT DIAGRAM

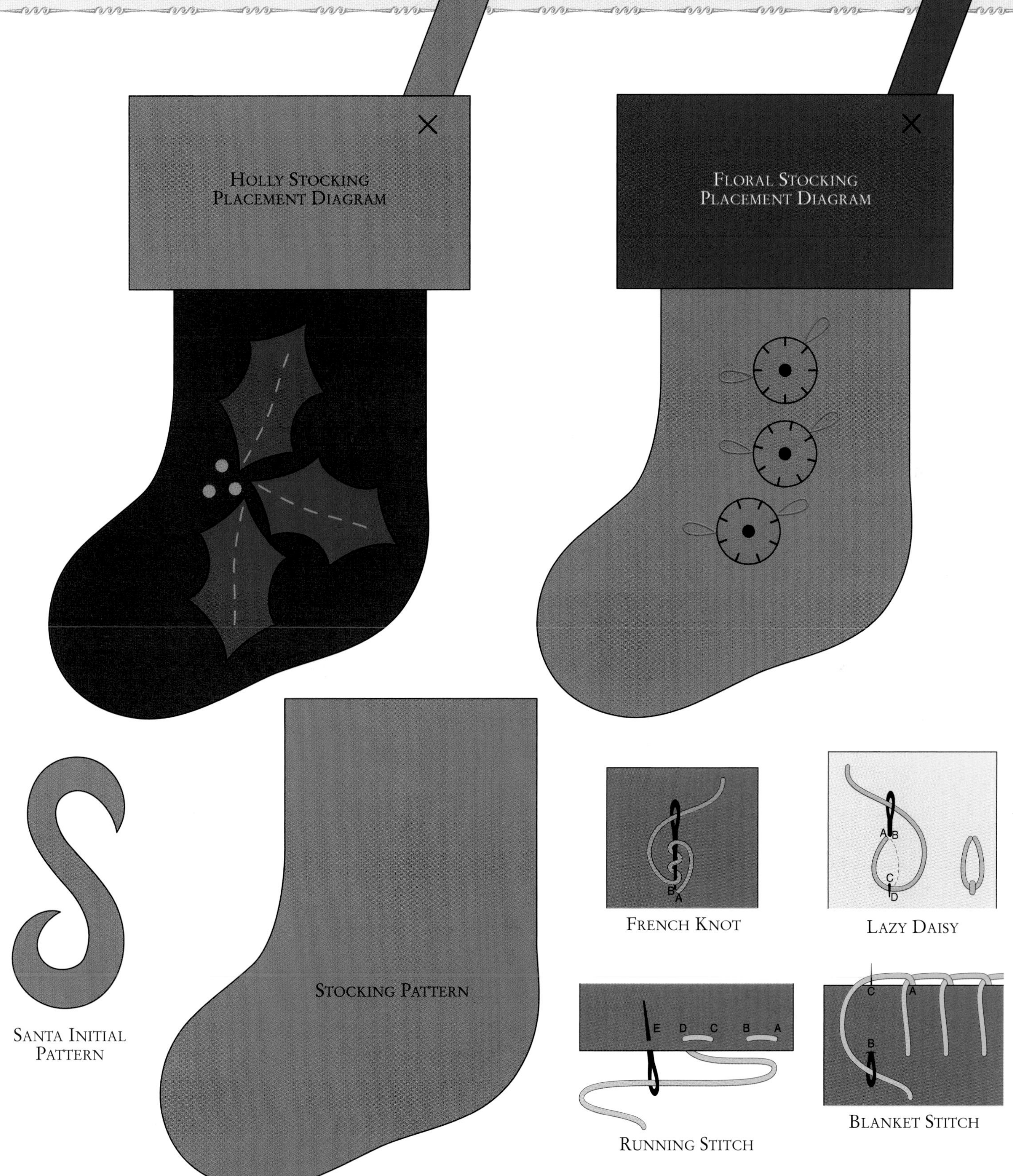
Holly Stocking
Placement Diagram
Floral Stocking
Placement Diagram
Santa Initial
Pattern
Stocking Pattern
B
A
French Knot
A B
C
D
Lazy Daisy
E D C B A
Running Stitch
C A
B
Blanket Stitch

Glistening Fruit Rings

A ring of miniature fruit with a dusting of frosty glitter decorates evergreen naturally.

WHAT YOU'LL NEED

Waxed paper
Miniature artificial fruit
Hot-glue gun; glue sticks
Paintbrush
White glue
White glitter
⅛-inch-wide gold ribbon
Scissors

WHAT TO DO

1 Cover the work surface with waxed paper. Arrange fruit pieces into a ring. Hot-glue the pieces together one at a time, keeping them flat on the work surface while working.

2 Brush white glue randomly over fruit ring. While the glue is wet, sprinkle with glitter. Let dry.

3 Cut a 12-inch length of ribbon. Thread through the fruit ring and tie the ribbon ends into a bow to create a hanger.

Sweet Stocking

Elegant with the rich and soft colors of brocade, this stocking ornament has button, braid, and ribbon accents.

WHAT YOU'LL NEED

Tracing paper; pencil; scissors
Mat board
Fleece
Thick white crafts glue
12-inch square of brocade fabric
Straight pins
6-inch square of contrasting fabric
¾ yard of ½-inch-wide flat braid
Matching thread
Needle
Buttons
Gold cord
18 inches of ribbon

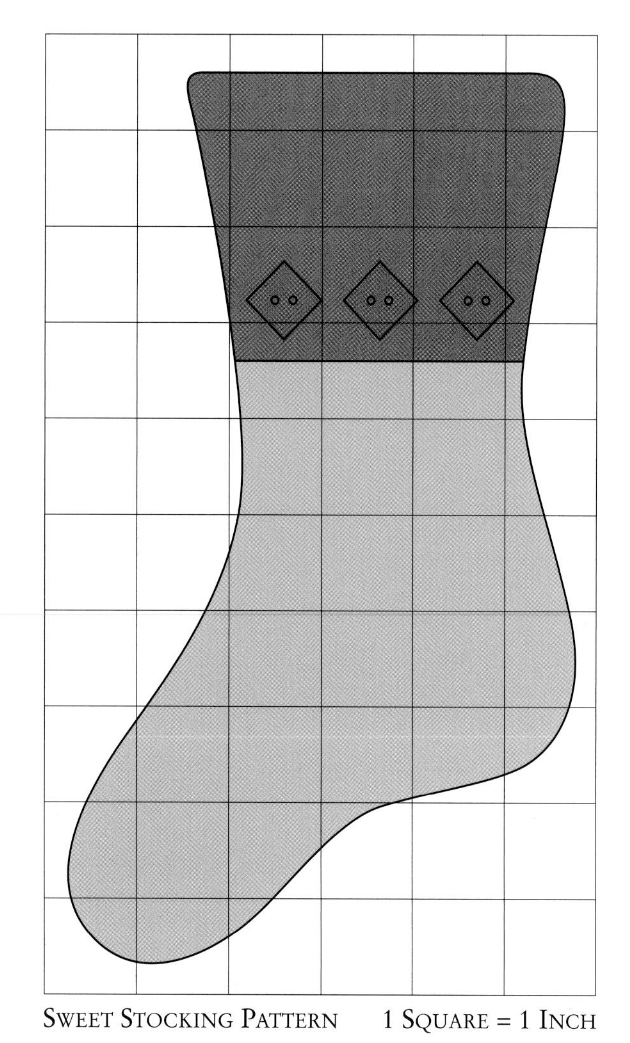

SWEET STOCKING PATTERN 1 SQUARE = 1 INCH

WHAT TO DO

1 Trace the pattern, *left*. Cut out shape. Trace around shape on mat board and cut out. Glue two layers of fleece on shape, trimming flush with edge of board.

2 Line brocade fabric with fleece stocking. Pin a paper pattern to the right side of the fabric. Straight-stitch around the edge. Cut out ornament ¾ inch beyond design.

3 Topstitch a contrasting band of fabric for cuff. Center the fabric over the mat board and glue the excess to the back side, clipping curves as necessary.

4 Glue braid around the stocking. Let dry. Sew on buttons. Stitch a cord hanging loop and ribbon bow to the right corner of the cuff.

Yarn Hooked Trims

Favorite motifs are created using lengths of wool in the age-old method of rug hooking.

What You'll Need

Tracing paper; transfer pen; scissors
Even-weave burlap fabric for rug hooking; hoop or frame
⅓ yard wool fabric or 12-inch lengths of wool scraps in the following colors:
snowman: white, black tweed, black, brown, and red
Orange yarn
snowflake: blue, white
mitten: red, green, white
Hook; thick white crafts glue
Mat board; wool felt; pinking shears
2 yards of cord; jingle bells

What To Do

1 Trace patterns, *pages 132–133,* and transfer to even-weave fabric, leaving at least 2 inches beyond the design. Cut wool into ¼- or ⅛-inch strips for finer detail.

2 To hook designs, mount even-weave fabric in hoop or frame. Hold one end of wool strip under even-weave fabric. Push hook between threads from top and pull end of wool through to right side as shown in Diagrams A and B, *right*. Move two threads and repeat, pulling a loop to right side. Keeping loop on hook, pull on wool from underside until loop is ⅛ inch tall as shown in Diagram C. Referring to patterns for colors, continue pulling up loops to cover entire area. Use ⅛-inch-wide cut wool fabric to outline each design area; fill in with ¼-inch-wide wool fabric; cut. Trim ends even with loops. Block finished design with a steam iron.

3 Trim even-weave fabric ½ inch beyond the design. Glue excess fabric to back side, clipping as necessary. Cut mat board the same shape as design and glue to back of design. Glue felt to back of mat board. Trim felt with pinking shears ¼ inch beyond the hooked design.

4 Glue cord along hooked edge and make a loop for hanging. Tie cord around loop into a bow. Add jingle bell trims. With pinking shears, cut a scrap of red wool for snowman's scarf and glue on.

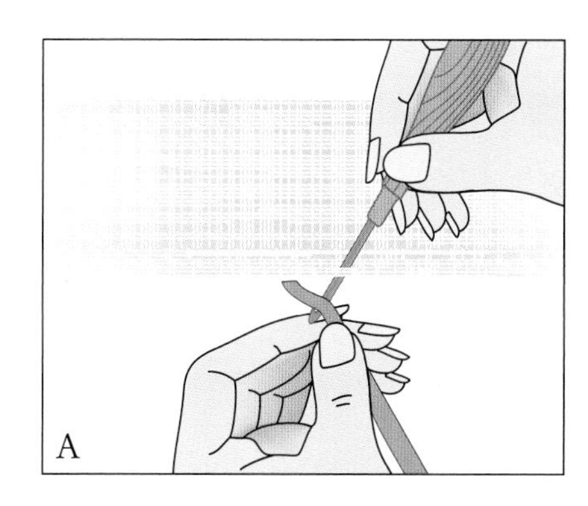

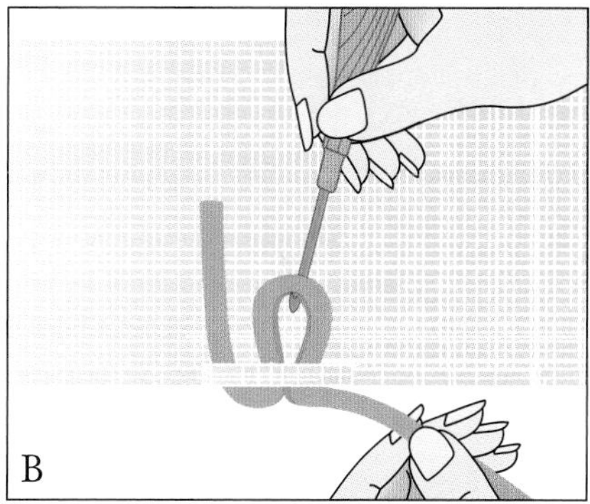

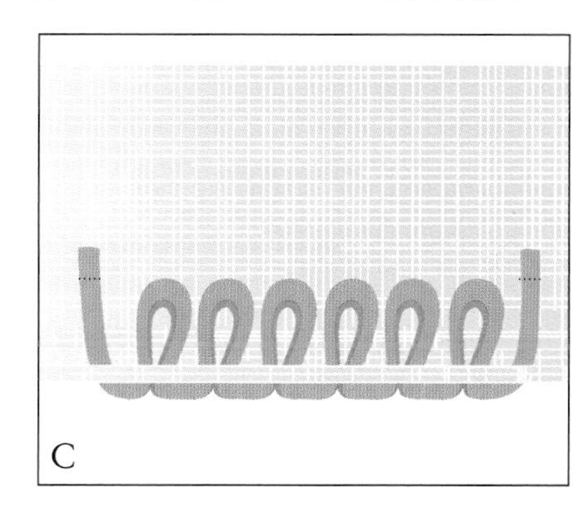

Yarn Hooked Trims continued

Snowflake Hooked Rug
Ornament Pattern

Snowman Hooked Rug
Ornament Pattern

Mitten Hooked Rug
Ornament Pattern

Flowering Star

Sequins and beads are the center attraction of this striking holiday star edged with piping-style cording. Use it as an ornament or as a sparkling tree topper.

What You'll Need

Tracing paper; pencil
Scissors
Heavy cardboard, such as chipboard
Thick quilt batting
Large scrap of stretch fabric
Straight pins
8-inch-square piece of felt
Bugle and seed beads
6 flower-shape sequins
Needle; thread
Fabric glue
Hot-glue gun; glue sticks
1 yard of cording to complement fabric color

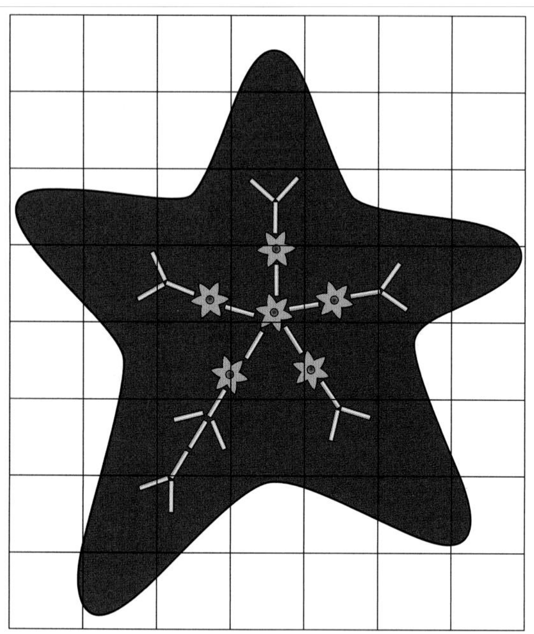

Star Pattern — 1 Square = 1 Inch

What To Do

1 Enlarge and trace the star pattern, *left*, and cut out. Trace around the pattern on cardboard. Cut out the cardboard shape.

2 Use the star pattern to cut a star shape from batting. Cut two 3-inch squares from batting. Stack the two squares on the center of the cardboard star. Dot glue on the batting star. Lay the batting star over the batting squares and glue it to the cardboard.

3 Cut the star from fabric ¼ inch larger than the pattern. To make cutting easier, make a series of cuts around inside curves of each star leg. Lay the fabric star over batting, matching the points. Pin the fabric to the center of the batting. Stretch fabric over cardboard edge, beginning at the inside curves, and gluing to cardboard back. Pull fabric over each point and glue in place. Finally, stretch and glue fabric along the sides of the points.

4 Cut a star from felt. Glue the felt star to the back of the fabric star, trimming away excess felt if necessary.

5 Begin beading in the center and work outward. With needle and thread, secure a seed bead to center of sequin to hold sequin in place. Use needle and thread to attach bugle beads.

6 Beginning at a point, use hot glue or fabric glue to attach cording to edge of star, leaving a tail at beginning and end. Tie the two tails together for a hanging loop.

Old-World St. Nick

French knots, running stitches, and straight stitches add texture and detail to felt shapes. A fiberfill center plumps this old-world St. Nick.

WHAT YOU'LL NEED

Tracing paper; pencil; scissors
Felt in gray, dark red, and ivory
Straight pins; embroidery floss in black and white; needle; fiberfill

WHAT TO DO

1 Trace and cut out patterns, *below*. Trace patterns on felt. Cut out two gray background pieces and one each of the three Santa pattern pieces.

2 Position and pin the face, hat, and shoulder pieces onto a background. Starting at the forehead of the face, use three plies of white floss to work French knots, *page 125*, along the edge of the felt, down the neck, and to fill the chin area. Work several French knots for the eyebrow and make straight stitches for the mustache using the diagram at *left*. Stitch a black French knot eye below the eyebrow. Remove pin.

3 Use three plies of black floss and running stitches to stitch the shoulder and hat pieces to the background. Stitch white Xs on the coat for buttons and along hat brim.

4 Make a wavy string of white French knots at the tip of the hat. Make five straight stitches at the end of the string to resemble a tassel.

5 Wrong sides together, stitch the curved top of the background piece to the backing piece using white floss and running stitches, *page 125*. Stuff the ornament with fiberfill. Sew the bottom edge closed. Secure a white floss loop at the top for hanging.

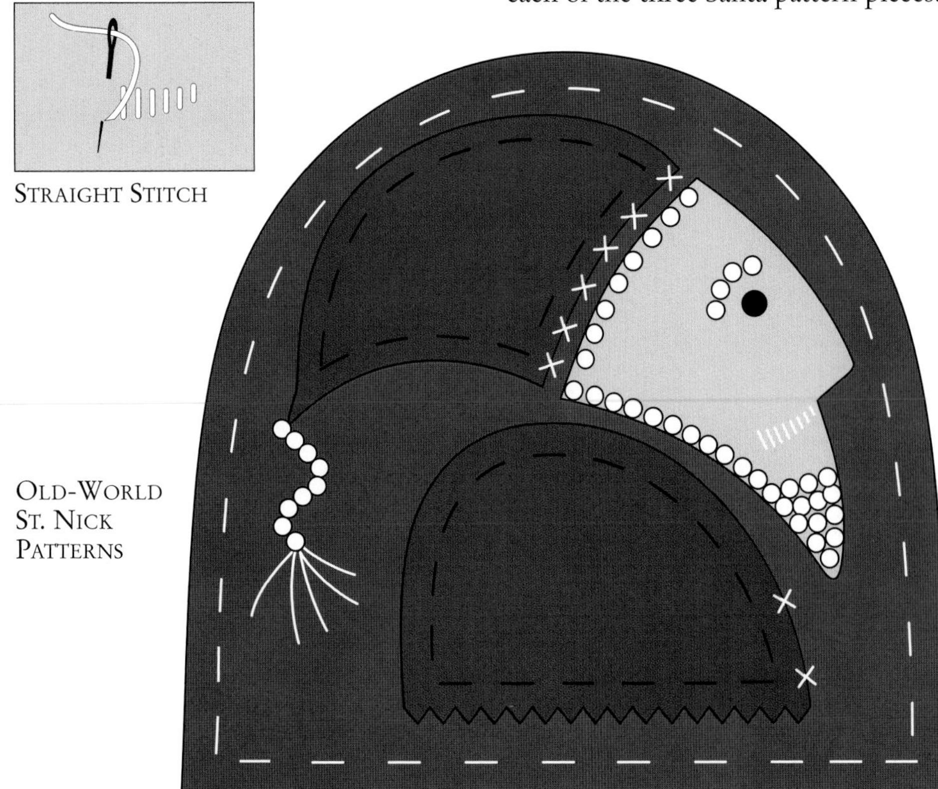

STRAIGHT STITCH

OLD-WORLD ST. NICK PATTERNS

Wired Rings

A silver snowflake charm dances center stage in rings of colorful metallic wire. The ornament hanger is given special attention by coiling the ends around a paintbrush.

What You'll Need

28-gauge metallic wire on spool in turquoise, bright pink, and silver
Wire cutters; silver snowflake charm
Cylinder shapes in 2½- and 1¼-inch diameters, such as wrapping paper tubes or tumblers

What To Do

1. Wrap the turquoise wire around the 2½-inch cylinder 16 times. Remove the wire from the cylinder. Use pink wire to wrap the turquoise circle.
2. Wrap the silver wire around the 1¼-inch cylinder 12 times. Remove the wire from the cylinder. Use turquoise wire to wrap the silver circle.
3. Cut an 18-inch length of wire for the hanger. Fold it in half. Slide the charm over one end of the hanger wire, sliding it to the fold. Twist the hanger wire three or four times to secure the charm. Slip the silver wire ring over one end of the hanger wire and twist several times to secure. Repeat with the turquoise ring. Twist the wire tails, leaving 1½ inches on each end. Shape the wire into a hanging loop, twist to secure. Wrap the wire tails around a paintbrush handle to form spirals.

Fruit Pails

A tiny silver pail holds holiday bounty and adds sparkle to traditional fruits.

WHAT YOU'LL NEED

Small silver pail
Table knife
Florist's foam
Miniature bright orange artificial kumquats
Sprigs of artificial red berries

WHAT TO DO

1 Cut a piece of florist's foam to fit the pail. Place the foam in the pail.

2 Insert kumquat stems and berries into the foam. Hang the ornament on the tree from the pail handle.

Recycle Christmas lightbulbs into a newfangled ornament that's as colorful as radiant stained glass windows.

WHAT YOU'LL NEED

Pencil; 2-inch plastic foam ball, such as Styrofoam
Six transparent colored standard-size Christmas lightbulbs
Thick white crafts glue
1 yard gold rickrack
Straight pins; 1 yard gold cording

WHAT TO DO

1 Mark six pencil dots equal distance apart on the plastic foam ball. Carefully twist each bulb into the foam at the dots. Remove a bulb, apply a dot of glue, and reinsert the bulb. Repeat for all of the bulbs. Let dry.

2 Secure an end of rickrack with a straight pin at the back of the ornament. Wrap the rickrack around the ball to cover the foam, ending at the starting point on the ball.

3 Wrap the cording over the rickrack and around every bulb. Secure with pins on the back of the ornament. Loop a piece of cording and pin it to the foam for a hanger.

Christmas Light

Ornament

Index

Sources

Batting
Morning Glory Products/ Division of Carpenter Co.

Mountain Mist/Stearns Technical
100 Williams St.
Cincinnati, OH 45215
800-543-7173
E-mail: mountain.mist@stearnstextiles.com
www.stearnstextiles.com

Beads
Gay Bowles Sales/Mill Hill
P.O. Box 1060
Janesville, WI 53547
www.millhill.com
800–356–9438

Westrim Trimming Corporation at 9667 Cantoga Avenue
Chatsworth, CA 91331
www.westrimcrafts.com
818–998–8550

Bodacious Beads
1942 River Road
Des Plaines, IL 84769-7959

Cross-Stitch Fabrics
Wichelt Imports, Inc.
N162 Hwy. 35
Stoddard, WI 54658

Zweigart
262 Old New Brunswick Road
Piscataway, NJ 08854
908–271–1949

Embroidery Floss
Anchor
Consumer Service Department
P.O. Box 27067
Greenville, SC 29616

DMC
Port Kearney Building 10
South Kearney, NJ 07032-0650

Fabrics
Bali Fabrics-Princess Mirah Design
800-783-4612
E-mail: BATIK@BALIFAB.COM
www.balifab.com

Benartex, Inc.
1359 Broadway
Suite 1100
New York, NY 10018
212-840-3250
www.benartex.com

Clothworks—A Division of Fabric Sales Co.
www.clothworks-fabrics.com

Cranston Printworks Co.
469 Seventh Avenue
New York, NY 10018
www.cranstonvillage.com

Dan River, Inc.
1065 Avenue of the Americas
New York, NY 10018

Fabri-Quilt, Inc.
901 E. 14th Ave.
N. Kansas City, MO 64116
www.fabri-quilt.com

Hoffmann California Fabrics
25792 Obrero Dr.
Mission Viejo, CA 92691
See local quilt shops for fabrics.

Marcus Brothers Textiles, Inc.
980 Avenue of the Americas
New York, NY 10018
212-354-8700
www.marcusbrothers.com

Moda/United Notions
13795 Hutton
Dallas, TX 75234
www.modafabrics.com

Northcott/Monarch
229 West 36th St.
New York, NY 10018
www.northcott.net

P & B Textiles
1580 Gilbreth Rd.
Burlingame, CA 94010
www.pbtex.com

Peter Pan Fabrics
11 East 36th St.
New York, NY 10016
800-854-5933

R.J.R. Fashion Fabrics
Purchased at local quilt shops.
To view complete fabric inventory, visit:
www.rjrfabrics.com

Notions
Prym-Dritz Corporation
P.O. Box 5028
Spartanburg, SC 29304

Ribbon
CM Offray & Son Inc.
Route 24, Box 601
Chester, NJ 07930-0601
908–879–4700

Projects Designers
Susan M. Banker—39, 64, 67, 71, 72, 74, 80–81, 91, 103, 121, 123, 137, 138
Carol Dahlstrom—8, 9, 10–11, 12, 13, 21, 25, 57, 59, 78, 108, 110, 112, 127, 141
Phyllis Dunstan—40–41, 135
Ardith Field—58
Wendy Elaine Johnson—109
Amy Jorgensen—97
Brenda Lesch—66
Alexa Lett—44–45, 65
Carrie Linder—51
Genevieve Mason—52–53
Margaret Sindelar—15, 17, 18–19, 22, 25, 31, 35, 46–47, 92, 93, 129, 131
Gayle Schadendorf—29, 79, 112, 113
Alice Wetzel—26–27, 33, 43, 63, 69, 77, 82, 99, 104, 107, 116–117

Photostyling
Carol Dahlstrom
Donna Chesnut, assistant

Hand Models
Jonathan Bailey, Lauren Bailey, Drew Carlson, Elizabeth Dahlstrom, Ardith Field, Kimberly Morris, and Alice Wetzel.